The Eleusinian and Bacchic Mysteries

The Eleusinian and Bacchic Mysteries
A Dissertation
Author: Thomas Taylor

Cover image: *Nymphs and Satyr (Pan),* 1873, William Bouguereau
Illustrations: A.L. Rawson
Lay-out: www.burokd.nl

ISBN 978-94-92355-29-4

© 2017 Revised publication by:

VAMzzz Publishing
P.O. Box 3340
1001 AC Amsterdam
The Netherlands
www.vamzzz.com
contactvamzzz@gmail.com

THE **ELEUSINIAN** AND **BACCHIC MYSTERIES**

A Dissertation

Thomas Taylor

VAMzzz PUBLISHING

Thomas Taylor
London, 15 May 1758 – Walworth, 1 November 1835)

contents

Εν ταις ΤΕΛΕΤΑΙΣ καθαρσεις ήγουνται και περιρράντηρια και αγνισμοι, ά των εν απορρήτοις δρωμενων, και της του θειου μετουσιας γυμνασματα εισιν.

Proclus: *Manuscript Commentary upon Plato, l. Alcibiades.*

Bacchic Ceremonies.

Bacchus and Nymphs.

Pluto, Proserpina, and Furies.

Eleusinian Priestesses.

Bacchante and Faun. Faun and Bacchus.

Eleusinian Mysteries.

Bacchus.

Fable is Love's World
– Poem by Schiller –

"'Tis not merely
The human being's pride that peoples space
With life and mystical predominance,
Since likewise for the stricken heart of Love
This visible nature, and this common world
Is all too narrow; yea, a deeper import
Lurks in the legend told my infant years
That lies upon that truth, we live to learn,
For fable is Love's world, his home, his birthplace;
Delightedly he dwells 'mong fays and talismans,
And spirits, and delightedly believes
Divinities, being himself divine.
The intelligible forms of ancient poets,
The fair humanities of Old Religion,
The Power, the Beauty, and the Majesty,
That had their haunts in dale or piny mountain,
Or forests by slow stream, or pebbly spring,
Or chasms or wat'ry depths;—all these have vanished.
They live no longer in the faith of Reason,
But still the heart doth need a language; still
Doth the old instinct bring back the old names."

Schiller: *The Piccolomini*, Act. ii. Scene 4.

Apollo and Muses.

Prometheus.

Introduction to the Third Edition

IN OFFERING TO the public a new edition of Mr. Thomas Taylor's admirable treatise upon the Eleusinian and Bacchic Mysteries, it is proper to insert a few words of explanation. These observances once represented the spiritual life of Greece, and were considered for two thousand years and more the appointed means for regeneration through an interior union with the Divine Essence. However absurd, or even offensive they may seem to us, we should therefore hesitate long before we venture to lay desecrating hands on what others have esteemed holy. We can learn a valuable lesson in this regard from the Grecian and Roman writers, who had learned to treat the popular religious rites with mirth, but always considered the Eleusinian Mysteries with the deepest reverence.

It is ignorance which leads to profanation. Men ridicule what they do not properly understand. Alcibiades was drunk when he ventured to touch what his countrymen deemed sacred. The undercurrent of this world is set toward one goal; and inside of human credulity—call it human weakness, if you please—is a power almost infinite, a holy faith capable of apprehending the supremest truths of all Existence. The veriest dreams of life, pertaining as they do to "the minor mystery of death," have in them more than external fact can reach or explain; and Myth, however much she is proved to be a child of Earth, is also received among men as the child of Heaven. The Cinder-Wench of the ashes will become the Cinderella of the Palace, and be wedded to the King's Son.

The instant that we attempt to analyze, the sensible, palpable facts upon which so many try to build disappear beneath the surface, like a foundation laid upon quicksand. "In the deepest reflections," says a distinguished writer, "all that we call external is only the material basis upon which our dreams are built; and the sleep that surrounds life swallows up life,—all but a dim wreck of matter, floating this way and that, and forever evanishing from sight. Complete the analysis, and we lose even the shadow of the external Present, and only the Past and the Future are left us as our sure inheritance. This is the first initiation,—the vailing [*muesis*] of the eyes to the external. But as *epoptæ*, by the synthesis of this Past and Future in a living nature, we obtain a higher, an ideal Present, comprehending within itself all that can be real for us within us or without. This is the second initiation in which is unvailed to us the Present as a new birth from our own life. Thus the great problem of Idealism is symbolically solved in the Eleusinia." [1]

These were the most celebrated of all the sacred orgies, and were called, by way of eminence, *The Mysteries*. Although exhibiting apparently the features of an Eastern origin, they were evidently copied from the rites of Isis in Egypt, an idea of which, more or less correct, may be found in *The Metamorphoses* of Apuleius and *The*

Epicurean by Thomas Moore. Every act, rite, and person engaged in them was symbolical; and the individual revealing them was put to death without mercy. So also was any uninitiated person who happened to be present. Persons of all ages and both sexes were initiated; and neglect in this respect, as in the case of Socrates, was regarded as impious and atheistical. It was required of all candidates that they should be first admitted at the *Mikra* or Lesser Mysteries of Agræ, by a process of fasting called *purification*, after which they were styled *mystæ*, or initiates. A year later, they might enter the higher degree. In this they learned the *aporrheta*, or secret meaning of the rites, and were thenceforth denominated *ephori*, or *epoptæ*. To some of the interior mysteries, however, only a very select number obtained admission. From these were taken all the ministers of holy rites. The Hierophant who presided was bound to celibacy, and required to devote his entire life to his sacred office. He had three assistants,—the torch-bearer, the *kerux* or crier, and the minister at the altar. There were also a *basileus* or king, who was an archon of Athens, four curators, elected by suffrage, and ten to offer sacrifices.

The sacred Orgies were celebrated on every fifth year; and began on the 15th of the month Boëdromian or September. The first day was styled the *agurmos* or assembly, because the worshipers then convened. The second was the day of purification, called also *aladé mystai*, from the proclamation: "To the sea, initiated ones!" The third day was the day of sacrifices; for which purpose were offered a mullet and barley from a field in Eleusis. The officiating persons were forbidden to taste of either; the offering was for *Achtheia* (the sorrowing one, Demeter) alone. On the fourth day was a solemn procession. The *kalathos* or sacred basket was borne, followed by women, *cistæ* or chests in which were sesamum, carded wool, salt, pomegranates, poppies,—also thyrsi, a serpent, boughs of ivy, cakes, etc. The fifth day was denominated the day of torches. In the evening were torchlight processions and much tumult.

Procession of Iacchos and Phallus.

The sixth was a great occasion. The statue of Iacchus, the son of Zeus and Demeter, was brought from Athens, by the *Iacchogoroi*, all crowned with myrtle. In the way was heard only an uproar of singing and the beating of brazen kettles, as the votaries danced and ran along. The image was borne "through the sacred Gate, along the sacred way, halting by the sacred fig-tree (all sacred, mark you, from Eleusinian associations), where the procession rests, and then moves on to the bridge over the Cephissus, where again it rests, and where the expression of the wildest grief gives place to the trifling farce,—even as Demeter, in the midst of her grief, smiled at the levity of Iambé in the palace of Celeus. Through the 'mystical entrance' we enter Eleusis. On the seventh day games are celebrated; and to the victor is given a measure of barley,—as it were a gift direct from the hand of the goddess. The eighth is sacred to Æsculapius, the Divine Physician, who heals all diseases; and in the evening is performed the initiatory ritual.

"Let us enter the mystic temple and be initiated,—though it must be supposed that, a year ago, we were initiated into the Lesser Mysteries at Agræ. We must have been *mystæ* (vailed), before we can become *epoptæ* (seers); in plain English, we must have shut our eyes to all else before we can behold the mysteries. Crowned with myrtle, we enter with the other initiates into the vestibule of the temple,—blind as yet, but the Hierophant within will soon open our eyes.

"But first,—for here we must do nothing rashly,—first we must wash in this holy water; for it is with pure hands and a pure heart that we are bidden to enter the most sacred enclosure [μυστικος σηκος, *mustikos sekos*]. Then, led into the presence of the Hierophant, [2] he reads to us, from a book of stone [πετρωμα, *petroma*], things which we must not divulge on pain of death. Let it suffice that they fit the place and the occasion; and though you might laugh at them, if they were spoken outside, still you seem very far from that mood now, as you hear the words of the old man (for old he he always was), and look upon the revealed symbols. And very far, indeed, are you from ridicule, when Demeter seals, by her own peculiar utterance and signals, by vivid coruscations of light, and cloud piled upon cloud, all that we have seen and heard from her sacred priest; and then, finally, the light of a serene wonder fills the temple, and we see the pure fields of Elysium, and hear the chorus of the Blessed;—then, not merely by external seeming or philosophic interpretation, but in real fact, does the Hierophant become the Creator [δημιουργος, *demiourgos*] and revealer of all things; the Sun is but his torch-bearer, the Moon his attendant at the altar, and Hermes his mystic herald [3] [κηρυξ, *kerux*]. But the final word has been uttered '*Conx Om pax*.' The rite is consummated, and we are *epoptæ* forever!"

Those who are curious to know the myth on which the "mystical drama" of the Eleusinia is founded will find it in any Classical Dictionary, as well as in these pages. It is only pertinent here to give some idea of the meaning. That it was regarded as profound is evident from the peculiar rites, and the obligations imposed on every initiated person. It was a reproach not to observe them. Socrates was accused of atheism, or disrespect to the gods, for having never been initiated. [4] Any person accidentally guilty of homicide, or of any crime, or convicted of witchcraft, was excluded. The secret doctrines, it is supposed, were the same as are expressed in the celebrated *Hymn* of Cleanthes. The philosopher Isocrates thus bears testimony: "She [Demeter] gave us two gifts that are the most excellent; fruits, that we may not live like beasts; and that initiation—those who have part in which have sweeter hope, both as regards the close of life and for all eternity." In like manner, Pindar also declares: "Happy is he who has beheld them, and descends into the Underworld: he knows the end, he knows the origin of life."

The Bacchic Orgies were said to have been instituted, or more probably reformed by Orpheus, a mythical personage, supposed to have flourished in Thrace. [5] The Orphic associations dedicated themselves to the worship of Bacchus, in which they hoped to find the gratification of an ardent longing after the worthy and elevating influences of a religious life. The worshipers did not indulge in unrestrained pleasure and frantic enthusiasm, but rather aimed at an ascetic purity of life and manners. The worship of Dionysus was the center of their ideas, and the starting-point of all their speculations upon the world and human nature. They believed that human souls were confined in the body as in a prison, a condition which was denominated *genesis* or generation; from which Dionysus would liberate them. Their sufferings, the stages by which they passed to a higher form of existence, their *katharsis* or purification, and their enlightenment constituted the themes of the Orphic writers. All this was represented in the legend which constituted the groundwork of the mystical rites.

Dionysus-Zagreus was the son of Zeus, whom he had begotten in the form of a dragon or serpent, upon the person of Kore or Persephoneia, considered by some to have been identical with Ceres or Demeter, and by others to have been her daughter. The former idea is more probably the more correct. Ceres or Demeter was called Koré at Cnidos. She is called Phersephatta in a fragment by Psellus, and is also styled a Fury. The divine child, an *avatar* or incarnation of Zeus, was denominated Zagreus, or Chakra (Sanscrit) as being destined to universal dominion. But at the instigation of Hera [6] the Titans conspired to murder him.

Etruscan Eleusinian Ceremonies.

Accordingly, one day while he was contemplating a mirror, [7] they set upon him, disguised under a coating of plaster, and tore him into seven parts. Athena, however, rescued from them his heart, which was swallowed by Zeus, and so returned into the paternal substance, to be generated anew. He was thus destined to be again born, to succeed to universal rule, establish the reign of happiness, and release all souls from the dominion of death.

The hypothesis of Mr. Taylor is the same as was maintained by the philosopher Porphyry, that the Mysteries constitute an illustration of the Platonic philosophy. At first sight, this may be hard to believe; but we must know that no pageant could hold place so long, without an under-meaning. Indeed, Herodotus asserts that "the rites called Orphic and Bacchic are in reality Egyptian and Pythagorean." [8] The influence of the doctrines of Pythagoras upon the Platonic system is generally acknowledged. It is only important in that case to understand the great philosopher correctly; and we have a key to the doctrines and symbolism of the Mysteries.

The first initiations of the Eleusinia were called *Teletæ* or terminations, as denoting that the imperfect and rudimentary period of generated life was ended and purged off; and the candidate was denominated a *mysta*, a vailed or liberated person. The Greater Mysteries completed the work; the candidate was more fully instructed and disciplined, becoming an *epopta* or seer. He was now regarded as having received the arcane principles of life. This was also the end sought by philosophy. The soul was believed to be of composite nature, linked on the one side to the eternal world, emanating from God, and so partaking of Divinity. On the other hand, it was also allied to the phenomenal or external world, and so liable to be subjected to passion, lust, and the bondage of evils. This condition is denominated *generation*; and is supposed to be a kind of death to the higher form of life. Evil is inherent in this condition; and the soul dwells in the body as in a prison or a grave. In this state, and previous to the discipline of education and the mystical initiation, the rational or intellectual element, which Paul denominates the spiritual, is asleep. The earth-life is a dream rather than a reality. Yet it has longings for a higher and nobler form of life, and its affinities are on high. "All men yearn after God," says Homer. The object of Plato is to present to us the fact that there are in the soul certain *ideas* or principles, innate and connatural, which are not derived from without, but are anterior to all experience, and are developed and brought to view, but not produced by experience. These ideas are the most vital of all truths, and the purpose of instruction and discipline is to make the individual conscious of them and willing to be led and inspired by them. The soul is purified or separated from evils by knowledge, truth, expiations, sufferings, and prayers. Our life is a discipline and preparation for another state of being; and resemblance to God is the highest motive of action. [9]

Proclus does not hesitate to identify the theological doctrines with the mystical dogmas of the Orphic system. He says: "What Orpheus delivered in hidden allegories, Pythagoras learned when he was initiated into the Orphic Mysteries; and Plato next received a perfect knowledge of them from the Orphean and Pythagorean writings."

Mr. Taylor's peculiar style has been the subject of repeated criticism; and his translations are not accepted by classical scholars. Yet they have met with favor at the hands of men capable of profound and recondite thinking; and it must be conceded that he was endowed with a superior qualification,—that of an intuitive perception of the interior meaning of the subjects which he considered. Others may have known more Greek, but he knew more Plato. He devoted his time and means for the elucidation and dissemination of the doctrines of the divine philosopher; and has rendered into English not only his writings, but also the works of other authors, who affected the teachings of the great master, that have escaped destruction at the hand of Moslem and Christian bigots. For this labor we cannot be too grateful.

The present treatise has all the peculiarities of style which characterize the translations. The principal difficulties of these we have endeavored to obviate—a labor which will, we trust, be not unacceptable to readers. The book has been for some time out of print; and no later writer has endeavored to replace it. There are many who still cherish a regard, almost amounting to veneration, for the author; and we hope that this reproduction of his admirable explanation of the nature and object of the Mysteries will prove to them a welcome undertaking. There is an increasing interest in philosophical, mystical, and other antique literature, which will, we believe, render our labor of some value to a class of readers whose sympathy, good-will, and fellowship we would gladly possess and cherish. If we have added to their enjoyment, we shall be doubly gratified.

A. W.

Venus and Proserpina in Hades.

Rape of Proserpina.

Pallas, Venus, and Diana.

FOOTNOTES

1. *Atlantic Monthly*, vol. iv. September, 1859.
2. In the Oriental countries the designation *Peter* (an interpreter), appears to have been the title of this personage; and the petroma consisted, notably enough, of two tablets of stone. There is in these facts some reminder of the peculiar circumstances of the Mosaic Law which was so preserved; and also of the claim of the Pope to be the successor of Peter, the hierophant or interpreter of the Christian religion.
3. Porphyry.
4. *Ancient Symbol-Worship*, page 12, note. "Socrates was not initiated, yet after drinking the hemlock, he addressed Crito: 'We owe a cock to Æsculapius.' This was the peculiar offering made by initiates (now called *kerknophori*) on the eve of the last day, and he thus symbolically asserted that he was about to receive the great apocalypse."
   See, also, *"Progress of Religious Ideas,"* by Lydia Maria Child, vol. ii. p. 308; and *"Discourses on the Worship of Priapus,"* by Richard Payne Knight.
5. Euripides: *Rhaesus*. "Orpheus showed forth the rites of the hidden Mysteries."
   Plato: *Protagoras*. "The art of a sophist or sage is ancient, but the men who proposed it in ancient times, fearing the odium attached to it, sought to conceal it, and vailed it over, some under the garb of poetry, as Homer, Hesiod, and Simonides: and others under that of the Mysteries and prophetic manias, such as Orpheus, Musæus, and their followers." Herodotus takes a different view—ii. 49. "Melampus, the son of Amytheon," he says, "introduced into Greece the name of Dionysus (Bacchus), the ceremonial of his worship, and the procession of the phallus. He did not, however, so completely apprehend the whole doctrine as to be able to communicate it entirely: but various sages, since his time, have carried out his teaching to greater perfection. Still it is certain that Melampus introduced the phallus, and that the Greeks learnt from him the ceremonies which they now practice. I therefore maintain that Melampus, who was a sage, and had acquired the art of divination, having become acquainted with the worship of Dionysus through knowledge derived from Egypt, introduced it into Greece, with a few slight changes, at the same time that he brought in various other practices. For I can by no means allow that it is by mere coincidence that the Bacchic ceremonies in Greece are so nearly the same as the Egyptian."
6. Hera, generally regarded as the Greek title of Juno, is not the definite name of any goddess, but was used by ancient writers as a designation only. It signifies *domina* or lady, and appears to be of Sanscrit origin. It is applied to Ceres or Demeter, and other divinities.
7. The mirror was a part of the symbolism of the Thesmophoria, and was used in the search for Atmu, the Hidden One, evidently the same as Tammuz, Adonis, and Atys. See *Exodus* xxxviii. 8; 1 *Samuel* ii. 22; and *Ezekiel* viii. 14. But despite the assertion of Herodotus and others that the Bacchic Mysteries were in reality Egyptian, there exists strong probability that they came originally from India, and were Sivaic or Buddhistical. Coré-Persephoneia was but the goddess Parasu-pani or Bhavani, the patroness of the Thugs, called also Gorée; and Zagreus is from *Chakra*, a country extending from ocean to ocean. If this is a Turanian or Tartar Story, we can easily recognize the "Horns" as the crescent worn by lama-priests: and translating god-names as merely sacerdotal designations, assume the whole legend to be based on a tale of Lama Succession and transmigration. The Titans would then be the Daityas of India, who were opposed to the faith of the northern tribes; and the title Dionysus but signify the god or chief-priest of

Nysa, or Mount Meru. The whole story of Orpheus, the institutor or rather the reformer of the Bacchic rites, has a Hindu ring all through.

8. HERODOTUS: ii. 81.
9. Many of the early Christian writers were deeply imbued with the Eclectic or Platonic doctrines. The very forms of speech were almost identical. One of the four Gospels, bearing the title "*according to John*," was the evident product of a Platonist, and hardly seems in a considerable degree Jewish or historical. The epistles ascribed to Paul evince a great familiarity with the Eclectic philosophy and the peculiar symbolism of the Mysteries, as well as with the Mithraic notions that had penetrated and permeated the religious ideas of the western countries.

SECTION I.

The Eleusinian Mysteries

DR. WARBURTON, IN HIS Divine Legation of Moses, has ingeniously proved, that the sixth book of Virgil's Æneid represents some of the dramatic exhibitions of the Eleusinian Mysteries; but, at the same time, has utterly failed in attempting to unfold their latent meaning, and obscure though important end. By the assistance, however, of the Platonic philosophy, I have been enabled to correct his errors, and to vindicate the wisdom [10] of antiquity from his aspersions by a genuine account of this sublime institution; of which the following observations are designed as a comprehensive view.

In the first place, then, I shall present the reader with two superior authorities, who perfectly demonstrate that a part of the shows (or dramas) consisted in a representation of the infernal regions; authorities which, though of the last consequence, were unknown to Dr. Warburton himself. The first of these is no less a person than the immortal Pindar, in a fragment preserved by Clemens Alexandrinus: "Ἀλλα και Πινδαρος περι των εν Ελευσινι μυστηριων λεγων επιφερει. Ολβιος, οστις ιδων εκεινα, κοινα εις ὑποχθονια, οιδεν μεν βιον τελευταν, οιδεν δε διος δοτον αρχαν." [11] *i. e.* "But Pindar, speaking of the Eleusinian Mysteries, says: Blessed is he who, having seen those *common concerns* in the underworld, knows both the end of life and its divine origin from Jupiter."

The other of these is from Proclus in his Commentary on Plato's *Politicus*, who, speaking concerning the sacerdotal and symbolical mythology, observes, that from this mythology Plato himself establishes many of his own peculiar doctrines, "since in the *Phædo* he venerates, with a becoming silence, the assertion delivered in the arcane discourses, that men are placed in the body as in a prison, secured by a guard, *and testifies, according to the mystic ceremonies, the different allotments of purified and unpurified souls in Hades, their severed conditions, and the three-forked path from the peculiar places where they were; and this was shown according to traditionary institutions; every part of which is full of a symbolical representation, as in a dream, and of a description which treated of the ascending and descending ways, of the tragedies of Dionysus (Bacchus or Zagreus), the crimes of the Titans, the three ways in Hades, and the wandering of everything of a similar kind."* — "Δηλοι δε εν Φαιδωνι τον τε εν απρρonτοις λεγομενον, ὡς εντινι φρουρα εσμεν ὁι ανθρωποι, σιγη τη τρεπουση σεβων, και τας τελετας (lege και κατα τας τελετα) μαρτυρομενος των διαφορων ληξεων της ψυχης κεκαθαρμενης τε και ακαθαρτου εις ᾁδου απιουσης, και τας τε σχεσεις αυ, και τας τριοδους απο των ουσιων και των (lege καί κατα των), πατρικων θεσμων τεκμαιρομενος. α δη της συμβολικης ᾁπαντα θεωριας εστι μεστα, και των παρα τοις ποιηταις θρυλλουμενων ανοδων τε και καθοδων, των τε διονυσιακων συνθηματων, και των τιτανικων ᾁμαρτηματων λεγομενων, και των εν ᾅδου τριοδων, και της πλανης, και των τοιουτων ἁπαντων." [12]

Having premised thus much, I now proceed to prove that the dramatic spectacles of the Lesser Mysteries [13] were designed by the ancient theologists, their founders, to signify occultly the condition of the unpurified soul invested with an earthly body, and enveloped in a material and physical nature; or, in other words, to signify that such a soul in the present life might be said to die, as far as it is possible for a soul to die, and that on the dissolution of the present body, while in this state of impurity, it would experience a death still more permanent and profound. That the soul, indeed, till purified by philosophy, [14] suffers death through its union with the body was obvious to the philologist Macrobius, who, not penetrating the secret meaning of the ancients, concluded from hence that they signified nothing more than the present body, by their descriptions of the infernal abodes. But this is manifestly absurd; since it is universally agreed, that all the ancient theological poets and philosophers incul-cated the doctrine of a future state of rewards and punishments in the most full and decisive terms; at the same time occultly intimating that *the death of the soul was nothing more than a profound union with the ruinous bonds of the body.*

Indeed, if these wise men believed in a future state of retribu-tion, and at the same time considered a connection with the body as death of the soul, it necessarily follows, that the soul's punishment and existence hereafter are nothing more than a continuation of its state at present, and a transmigration, as it were, from sleep to sleep, and from dream to dream. But let us attend to the assertions of these divine men concerning the soul's union with a material nature. And to begin with the obscure and profound Heracleitus, speaking of souls unembodied: "We live their death, and we die their life." Ζωμεν τον εκεινων θανατον, τεθνηκαμεν δε τον εκεινων βιον. And Empedocles, deprecating the condition termed "generation," beautifully says of her:

> The aspect changing with destruction dread,
> She makes the *living* pass into the *dead*.
> Εκ μεν γαρ ζωων ετιθει νεκρα ειδε αμειβων.

And again, lamenting his connection with this corporeal world, he pathetically exclaims:

> For this I weep, for this indulge my woe,
> That e'er my soul such novel realms should know.
> Κλαυσα τε και κωκυσα, ὦων ασυνηθεα χωρον.

Plato, too, it is well known, considered the body as the sepulchre of the soul, and in the *Cratylus* concurs with the doctrine of Orpheus, that the soul is punished through its union with body. This was likewise the opinion of the celebrated Pythagorean, Philolaus, as is evident from the following remarkable passage in the Doric dialect, preserved by Clemens Alexandrinus in *Stromat.* book iii. "Μαρτυρεοντα δε και οι παλαιοι θεολογοι τε και μαντιες, ὡς δια τινας τιμωριας, ἁ ψυχα τῷ σωματι συνεζευκται, και καθαπερ εν σωματι τομτῳ τεθαπται." *i. e.* "The ancient theologists and priests [15] also testify that the soul is united with the body as if for the sake of punishment; [16] and so is buried in body as in a sepulchre." And, lastly, Pythagoras himself confirms the above sentiments, when he beautifully observes, according to Clemens in the same book, "that *whatever we see when awake is death; and when asleep, a dream.*" θανατος εστιν, οκοσα εγερθεντες ορεομεν· οκοσα δε ευδοντες, ὑπνος.

But that the mysteries occultly signified this sublime truth, that the soul by being merged in matter resides among the dead both here and hereafter, though it follows by a necessary sequence from the preceding observations, yet it is indisputably confirmed, by the testimony of the great and truly divine Plotinus, in *Ennead* l., book viii. "When the soul," says he, "has descended into generation (from its first divine condition) she partakes of evil, and is carried a great way into a state the opposite of her first purity and integrity, *to be entirely merged in which, is nothing more than to fall into dark mire.*" And again, soon after: "The soul therefore *dies* as much as it is possible for the soul to die: *and the death to her is while baptized or immersed in the present body, to descend into matter,* [17] *and be wholly subjected by it; and after departing thence to lie there till it shall arise and turn its face away from the abhorrent filth. This is what is meant by the falling asleep in Hades, of those who have come there.*" [18] Γινομενῳ δε ἡ μεταληψις αυτου. Γιψνεται γαρ πανταπασιν εν τῳ της ανομοιοτητος τοπῳ, ενθα δυς εις αυτην εις βορβορον σκοτεινον εσται πεσων.—Αποθνησκει ουν, ως ψυχη αν θανοι· και ὁ θανατος αυτη, και ετι εν τω σωματι βεβαπτισμενη, εν ὑλη εστι καταδυναι, και πλησθηναι αυτης. Και εξελθουσης εκει κεισθαι, εως αναδραμη και αφελη πως την οψιν εκ του βορβορου. Και τουτο εστι το εν ᾁδου ελθοντα επικατα δαρθειν.

Narcissus. Herse and Mercury.

Here the reader may observe that the obscure doctrine of the Mysteries mentioned by Plato in the *Phædo*, that the unpurified soul in a future state lies immerged in mire, is beautifully explained; at the same time that our assertion concerning their secret meaning is not less substantially confirmed. [19] In a similar manner the same divine philosopher, in his book on the Beautiful, *Ennead*, I., book vi., explains the fable of Narcissus as an emblem of one who rushes to the contemplation of sensible (phenomenal) forms as if they were perfect realities, when at the same time they are nothing more than like beautiful images appearing in water, fallacious and vain. "Hence," says he, "as Narcissus, by catching at the shadow, plunged himself in the stream and disappeared, so he who is captivated by beautiful bodies, and does not depart from their embrace, is precipitated, not with his body, but with his soul, into a darkness profound and repugnant to intellect (the higher soul), [20] through which, remaining blind both here and in Hades, he associates with shadows." Τον αυτον δη τροπον ὁ εχομενος των καλων σωμα των, και μη αφιεις, ου τῳ σωματι, τῃ δε ψυχῃ καταδυσεται, εις σκοτεινα και ατερπη τῳ νῳ βαθη, ενθα τυφλος εν ᾁδου μενων, και ενταυθα κᾁκει σκιαις συνεστι. And what still farther confirms our exposition is that matter was considered by the Egyptians as a certain mire or mud. "The Egyptians," says Simplicius, "called matter, which they symbolically denominated water, the dregs or sediment of the first life; matter being, as it were, a certain mire or mud. [21] Διο και Αιγυπτιοι την της πρωτης ζωης, ἡν ὑδωρ συμβολικως εκαλουν, ὑποσταθμην την ὑλην ελεγον, ὁιον ιλον τινα ουσαν. So that from all that has been said we may safely conclude with Ficinus, whose words are as express to our purpose as possible. "Lastly," says he, "that I may comprehend the opinion of the ancient theologists, on the state of the soul after death, in a few words: *they considered*, as we have elsewhere asserted, *things divine as the only realities, and that all others were only the images and shadows of truth.* Hence they asserted that prudent men, who earnestly employed themselves in divine concerns, were above all others in a vigilant state. But that imprudent [*i. e.* without foresight] men, who pursued objects of a different nature, being laid asleep, as it were, were only engaged in the delusions of dreams; and that if they happened to die in this sleep, before they were roused, they would be afflicted with similar and still more dazzling visions in a future state. And that as he who in this life pursued realities, would, after death, enjoy the highest truth, so he who pursued deceptions would hereafter be tormented with fallacies and delusions in the extreme: as the one would be delighted with true objects of enjoyment, so the other would be tormented with delusive semblances of reality."—Denique ut priscorum theologorum sententiam de statu animæ post mortem paucis comprehendam: sola divina (ut alias diximus) arbitrantur res veras existere, reliqua esse rerum verarum imagines atque umbras. Ideo prudentes homines, qui divinis incumbunt, præ ceteris vigilare. Imprudentes autem, qui sectantur alia, insomniis omnino quasi dormientes illudi, ac si in hoc somno priusquam expergefacti fuerint moriantur similibus post discessum et acrioribus visionibus angi. Et sicut eum qui in vita veris incubuit, post mortem summa veritate potiri, sic eum qui falsa sectatus est, fallacia extrema torqueri, ut ille rebus veris oblectetur, hic falsis vexetur simulachris." [22]

But notwithstanding this important truth was obscurely hinted by the Lesser Mysteries, we must not suppose that it was generally known even to the initiated persons themselves: for as individuals of almost all descriptions were admitted to these rites, it would have been a ridiculous prostitution to disclose to the multitude a theory so abstracted and sublime. [23] It was sufficient to instruct these in the doctrine of a future state of rewards and punishments, and in the means of returning to the principles from which they originally fell: for this last piece of information was, according to Plato in the *Phædo*, the ultimate design of the Mysteries; and the former is necessarily inferred from the present discourse. Hence the reason why it was obvious to none but the Pythagorean and Platonic philosophers, who derived their theology from Orpheus himself, [24] the original founder of these sacred institutions; and why we meet with no information in this particular in any writer prior to Plotinus; as he was the first who, having penetrated the profound interior wisdom of antiquity, delivered it to posterity without the concealments of mystic symbols and fabulous narratives.

Virgil not a Platonist

Hence too, l think, we may infer, with the greatest probability, that this recondite meaning of the Mysteries was not known even to Virgil himself, who has so elegantly described their external form; for notwithstanding the traces of Platonism which are to be found in the *Æneid*, nothing of any great depth occurs throughout the whole, except what a superficial reading of Plato and the dramas of the Mysteries might easily afford. But this is not perceived by modern readers, who, entirely unskilled themselves in Platonism, and fascinated by the charms of his poetry, imagine him to be deeply knowing in a subject with which he was most likely but slightly acquainted. This opinion is still farther strengthened by considering that the doctrine delivered in his *Eclogues* is perfectly Epicurean, which was the fashionable philosophy of the Augustan age; and that there is no trace of Platonism in any other part of his works but the present book, which, containing a representation of the Mysteries, was necessarily obliged to display some of the principal tenets of this philosophy, so far as they illustrated and made a part of these mystic exhibitions. However, on the supposition that this book presents us with a faithful view of some part of these sacred rites, and this accompanied with the utmost elegance, harmony, and purity of versification, it ought to be considered as an invaluable relic of antiquity, and a precious monument of venerable mysticism, recondite wisdom, and theological information. [25] This will be sufficiently evident from what has been already delivered, by considering some of the beautiful descriptions of this book in their natural order; at the same time that the descriptions themselves will corroborate the present elucidations.

In the first place, then, when he says,

—facilis descensus Averno.
Noctes atque dies patet atra janua ditis:
Sed revocare gradum, superasque evadere ad auras,
Hoc opus, hic labor est. Pauci quos æquus amavit
Jupiter, aut ardens evexit ad æthera virtus,
Dis geniti potuere. Tenent media omnia silvæ,
Cocytusque sinu labens, circumvenit atro—†

† *Davidson's Translation.*—"Easy is the path that leads down to hell; grim Pluto's gate stands open night and day: but to retrace one's steps, and escape to the upper regions, this is a work, this is a task. Some few, whom favoring Jove loved, or illustrious virtue advanced to heaven, the sons of the gods, have effected it. Woods cover all the intervening space, and

Cocytus, gliding with his black, winding flood, surrounds it."

is it not obvious, from the preceding explanation, that by Avernus, in this place, and the dark gates of Pluto, we must understand a corporeal or external nature, the descent into which is, indeed, at all times obvious and easy, but to recall our steps, and ascend into the upper regions, or, in other words, to separate the soul from the body by the purifying discipline, is indeed a mighty work, and a laborious task? For a few only, the favorites of heaven, that is, born with the true philosophic genius, [26] and whom ardent virtue has elevated to a disposition and capacity for divine contemplation, have been enabled to accomplish the arduous design. But when he says that all the middle regions are covered with woods, this likewise plainly intimates a material nature; the word *silva*, as is well known, being used by ancient writers to signify matter, and implies nothing more than that the passage leading to the *barathrum* [abyss] of body, *i. e.* into profound darkness and oblivion, is through the medium of a material nature; and this medium is surrounded by the black bosom of Cocytus, [27] that is, by bitter weeping and lamentations, the necessary consequence of the soul's union with a nature entirely foreign to her own. So that the poet in this particular perfectly corresponds with Empedocles in the line we have cited above, where he exclaims, alluding to this union,

For this I *weep*, for this *indulge my woe*,
That e'er my soul such novel realms should know.
In the next place, he thus describes the cave, through which

Æneas descended to the infernal regions:

> Spelunca alta fuit, vastoque immanis hiatu,
> Scrupea, tuta lacu nigro, memorumque tenebris:
> Quam super hand ullæ poterant impune volantes
> Tendere iter pennis: talis sese halitus atris
> Faucicus effundens supera ad convexa ferebat:
> Unde locum Graii dixerunt nomine Aornum–†

† *Davidson's Translation.*—"There was a cave profound and hideous, with wide yawning mouth, stony, fenced by a black lake, and the gloom of woods; over which none of the flying kind were able to wing their way unhurt; such exhalations issuing from its grim jaws ascended to the vaulted skies; for which reason the Greeks called the place by the name of *Aornos*" (without birds). [28]

Does it not afford a beautiful representation of a corporeal nature, of which a cave, defended with a black lake, and dark woods, is an obvious emblem? For it occultly reminds us of the ever-flowing and obscure condition of such a nature, which may be said

> To roll incessant with impetuous speed,
> Like some dark river, into Matter's sea.

Nor is it with less propriety denominated *Aornus, i. e.* destitute of birds, or a winged nature; for on account of its native sluggishness and inactivity, and its merged condition, being situated in the outmost extremity of things, it is perfectly debile and languid, incapable

42

of ascending into the regions of reality, and exchanging its obscure and degraded station for one every way splendid and divine. The propriety too of sacrificing, previous to his entrance, to Night and Earth, is obvious, as both these are emblems of a corporeal nature.

In the verses which immediately follow,—

Ecce autem, primi sub limina solis et ortus,
Sub pedibus mugire solum, et juga cæpta movere
Silvarum, visaque canes ululare per umbram,
Adventante dea–[*]

we may perceive an evident allusion to the earthquakes, etc., attending the descent of the soul into body, mentioned by Plato in the tenth book of his *Republic;* [29] since the lapse of the soul, as we shall see more fully hereafter, was one of the important truths which these Mysteries were intended to reveal. And the howling dogs are symbols of material [30] demons, who are thus denominated by the *Magian Oracles* of Zoroaster, on account of their ferocious and malevolent dispositions, ever baneful to the felicity of the human soul. And hence Matter herself is represented by Synesius in his first *Hymn*, with great propriety and beauty, as barking at the soul with devouring rage: for thus he sings, addressing himself to the Deity:

Μακαρ ός τις βορον ύλας

---

* "So, now, at the first beams and rising of the sun, the earth under the feet begins to rumble, the wooded hills to quake, and dogs were seen howling through the shade, as the goddess came hither–"

Προφυγων ὑλαγμα, και γας

Αναδυς, ἁλματι κουφῳ

Ιχνος ες θεον τιταινει.

Which may be thus paraphrased:

Blessed! thrice blessed! who, with wingéd speed,

From Hylé's [31] dread voracious barking flies,

And, leaving Earth's obscurity behind,

By a light leap, directs his steps to thee.

And that material demons actually appeared to the initiated previous to the lucid visions of the gods themselves, is evident from the following passage of Proclus in his manuscript *Commentary on the first Alcibiades:* εν ταις ἁγιοταταις των τελετων τρο της θεου παρουσιας δαιμονων χθονιων εκβολαι προφαινονται, και απο των αχραντων αγαθων εις την ὑλην προκαλουμεναι. *I. e.* "In the most interior sanctities of the Mysteries, before the presence of the god, the rushing forms of earthly demons appear, and call the attention from the immaculate good to matter." And Pletho (*on the Oracles*), expressly asserts, that these spectres appeared in the shape of dogs.

After this, Æneas is described as proceeding to the infernal regions, through profound night and darkness:

Ibant obscuri sola sub nocte per umbram.

Perque domos Ditis vacuas, et inania regna.

Quale per incertam lunam sub luce maligna

Est iter in silvis: ubi cælum condidit umbra
Jupiter, et rebus nox abstulit atra colorem.[*]

And this with the greatest propriety; for the Mysteries, as is well known, were celebrated by night; and in the Republic of Plato, as cited above, souls are described as falling into the estate of generation at midnight; this period being peculiarly accommodated to the darkness and oblivion of a corporeal nature; and to this circumstance the nocturnal celebration of the Mysteries doubtless alluded.

In the next place, the following vivid description presents itself to our view:

Vestibulum ante ipsum, primisque in faucibus Orci
Luctus, et ultrices posuere cubilia Curæ:
Pallentesque habitant morbi, tristisque senectus,
Et Metus, et mala suada Fames, ac turpis egestas;
Terribiles visu formæ; Lethumque Laborque;
Tum consanguineus Lethi Sopor et mala mentis
Gaudia, mortiferumque adverso in limine bellum
Ferreique Eumenidum thalami et Discordia demens,
Vipereum crinem vittis innexa cruentis.
In medio ramos annosaque brachia pandit
Ulmus opaca ingens: quam sedem somnia vulgo

---

* "They went along, amid the gloom under the solitary night, through the shade, and through the desolate halls, and empty realms of Dis [Pluto or Hades]. Such is a journey in the woods beneath the unsteady moon with her niggard light, when Jupiter has enveloped the sky in shade, and the black Night has taken from all objects their color."

Vana tenere ferunt, foliisque sub omnibus hærent.

Multaque præterea variarum monstra ferarum:

Centauri in foribus stabulant, Scyllæque biformes,

Et centumgeminus Briareus, ac bellua Lernæ,

Horrendum stridens, flammisque armata Chimæra,

Gorgones Harpyiæque, et formo tricorporis umbræ.[*]

And surely it is impossible to draw a more lively picture of the maladies with which a material nature is connected; of the soul's dormant condition through its union with body; and of the various mental diseases to which, through such a conjunction, it becomes unavoidably subject; for this description contains a threefold division; representing, in the first place, the external evil with which this material region is replete; in the second place, intimating that the life of the soul when merged in the body is nothing but a dream; and, in the third place, under the disguise of multiform and terrific monsters, exhibiting the various vices of our irrational and sensuous part. Hence Empedocles, in perfect conformity with the first part of this description, calls this material abode, or the realms of generation,—ατερπεα χωρον, [32] a *"joyless region."*

---

* "Before the entrance itself, and in the first jaws of Hell, Grief and vengeful Cares have placed their couches; pale Diseases inhabit there, and sad Old Age, and Fear, and Want, evil goddess of persuasion, and unsightly Poverty—forms terrible to contemplate! and there, too, are Death and Toil; then Sleep, akin to Death, and evil Delights of mind; and upon the opposite threshold are seen death-bringing War, and the iron marriage-couches of the Furies, and raving Discord, with her viper-hair bound with gory wreaths. In the midst, an Elm dark and huge expands its boughs and aged limbs; making an abode which vain Dreams are said to haunt, and under whose every leaf they dwell. Besides all these, are many monstrous apparitions of various wild beasts. The Centaurs harbor at the gates, and double-formed Scyllas, the hundred-fold Briareus, the Snake of Lerna, hissing dreadfully, and Chimæra armed with flames, the Gorgons and the Harpies, and the shades of three-bodied form."

"Where slaughter, rage, and countless ills reside;
Ενθα φονος τε κοτος τε και αλλων εθνεα κηρων—

and into which those who fall,

"Through Até's meads and dreadful darkness stray."
Ατης ανα λειμωνα τε και σκοτος ηλασκουσιν.

And hence he justly says to such a soul, that

"She flies from deity and heav'nly light,
To serve *mad Discord* in the realms of night."
φυγας θεοθεν, και αλητης,
Νεικεϊ μαινομενῳ πισυνος.

Where too we may observe that the *Discordia demens* of Virgil is an exact translation of the Νεικεϊ μαινομενῳ of Empedocles.

In the lines, too, which immediately succeed, the sorrows and mournful miseries attending the soul's union with a material nature, are beautifully described.

Hinc via, Tartarei quæ fert Acherontis ad undas;
Turbidus hic cæno vastaque voragine gurges
Æstuat, atque omnem Cocyto eructat arenam.[*]

---

*   "Here is the way which leads to the surging billows of Hell [Acheron]; here an abyss turbid boils up with loathsome mud and vast whirlpools; and vomits all its quicksand into Cocytus."

Jupiter as Diana and Callisto.

Diana and Calisto.

And when Charon calls out to Æneas to desist from entering any farther, and tells him,

"Here to reside delusive shades delight;
"For nought dwells here but sleep and drowsy night."
Umbrarum hic locus est, Somni Noctisque soporæ—

nothing can more aptly express the condition of the dark regions of body, into which the soul, when descending, meets with nothing but shadows and drowsy night: and by persisting in her course, is at length lulled into profound sleep, and becomes a true inhabitant of the phantom-abodes of the dead.

Æneas having now passed over the Stygian lake, meets with the three-headed monster Cerberus, [33] the guardian of these infernal abodes:

Tandem trans fluvium incolumis vatemque virumque
Informi limo glaucaque exponit in ulva.

. . .

Cerberus hæc ingens latratu regna trifauci
Personat, adverso recubans immanis in antro.[*]

By Cerberus we must understand the discriminative part of the soul, of which a dog, on account of its sagacity, is an emblem;

---

* "At length across the river safe, the prophetess and the man, he lands upon the slimy strand, upon the blue sedge. Huge Cerberus makes these realms [of death] resound with barking from his threefold throat, as he lies stretched at prodigious length in the opposite cave."

and the three heads signify the triple distinction of this part, into the intellective [or intuitional], cogitative [or rational], and opinionative powers.—With respect [34] to the three kinds of persons described as situated on the borders of the infernal realms, the poet doubtless intended by this enumeration to represent to us the three most remarkable characters, who, though not apparently deserving of punishment, are yet each of them similarly immerged in matter, and consequently require a similar degree of purification. The persons described are, as is well known, first, the souls of infants snatched away by untimely ends; secondly, such as are condemned to death unjustly; and, thirdly, those who, weary of their lives, become guilty of suicide. And with respect to the first of these, or infants, their connection with a material nature is obvious. The second sort, too, who are condemned to death unjustly, must be supposed to represent the souls of men who, though innocent of one crime for which they were wrongfully punished, have, notwithstanding, been guilty of many crimes, for which they are receiving proper chastisement in Hades, *i. e.* through a profound union with a material nature. [35] And the third sort, or suicides, though apparently separated from the body, have only exchanged one place for another of similar nature; since conduct of this kind, according to the arcana of divine philosophy, instead of separating the soul from its body, only restores it to a condition perfectly correspondent to its former inclinations and habits, lamentations and woes. But if we examine this affair more profoundly, we shall find that these three characters are justly placed in the same situation, because the reason of punishment is in each equally obscure. For is it not a just matter of doubt why the souls of infants should be punished? And is it not equally dubious and wonderful why those who have been unjustly condemned to death in one period of existence should be punished in another? And as to suicides, Plato in his *Phædo* says that the prohibition of this crime in the απορρητα (*aporrheta*) [36] is a profound doctrine, and not easy to be understood. [37] Indeed, the true cause why the two first of these characters are in Hades, can only be ascertained from the fact of a prior state of existence, in surveying which, the latent justice of punishment will be manifestly revealed; the apparent inconsistencies in the administration of Providence fully reconciled; and the doubts concerning the wisdom of its proceedings entirely dissolved. And as to the last of these, or suicides, since the reason of their punishment, and why an action of this kind is in general highly atrocious, is extremely mystical and obscure, the following solution of this difficulty will, no doubt, be gratefully received by the Platonic reader, as the whole of it is no where else to be found but in manuscript. Olympiodorus, then, a most learned and excellent commentator on Plato, in his commentary on that part of the *Phædo* where Plato speaks of the prohibition of suicide in the *aporrheta*, observes as follows: "The argument which Plato employs in this place against suicide is derived from the Orphic mythology, in which four kingdoms are celebrated; the first of Uranus [Ouranos] (Heaven), whom Kronos or Saturn assaulted, cutting off the genitals of his father. [38] But after Saturn, Zeus or Jupiter succeeded to the government of the world, having hurled his father into Tartarus. And after Jupiter, Dionysus or Bacchus rose to light, who, according to report, was, through the insidious treachery of Hera or Juno, torn in pieces by the Titans, by whom he was surrounded, and who afterwards tasted his flesh: but Jupiter, enraged at the deed, hurled his thunder at the guilty offenders and consumed them to ashes. Hence a certain matter being formed from the ashes or sooty vapor of the smoke ascending from their burning bodies, out of this mankind were produced. It is unlawful, therefore, to destroy ourselves, not as the words of Plato seem to import, because we are in the body, as in prison, secured by a guard (for this is evident, and Plato would not have called such an assertion arcane), but because our body is Dionysiacal, [39] or of the nature of Bacchus: for we are a part of him, since we are composed from the ashes, or sooty vapor of the Titans who tasted his flesh. Socrates, therefore, as if fearful of disclosing the arcane part of this narration, relates nothing more of the fable than that we are placed as in a prison secured by a guard: but the interpreters relate the fable openly."

Και εςτι το μυθικον επιχειρημα τοιουτον. Παρα τω Ορφει τεσσαρες βασιλειαι παραδιδονται. Πρωτη μεν, ή του Ουρανου, ήν ό Κρονος διεδεξατο, εκτεμων τα αιδοια του πατρος. Μετα δη τον Κρονον, ό Ζευς εβασιλευσεν καταταρταρώσας τὸν πατερα. Ειτα τον Δια διεδεξατο ό Διονυσος, όν φασι κατ' επιβουλην της Ήρας τους περι αυτου Τιτανας σπαραττειν, και των σαρκων αυτου απογευεσθαι. Και τουτους οργισθεις ό Ζευς εκεραυνωσε, και εκ της αιθαλης των ατμων των αναδοθεντων εξ αυτων, ύλης γενομενης γενεσθαι τους ανθρωπους. Ου δει ουν εξαγαγειν ήμας εαυτους, ουχ οτι ως δοκει λεγειν ή λεξις, διοτι εν τινι δεσμω εσμεν τω σωματι· τουτο γαρ δηλον εστι, και ουκ αν τουτο απορρμτον ελεγε, αλλ' οτι ου δει εξαγαγειν ήμας έαυτους ως του σωματος ήμων διονυσιακου οντος· μερος γαρ αυτου εσμεν, ειγε εκ της αιθαλης των Τιτανων συγκειμεθα γευσαμενων των σαρκων τουτου. Ὁ μεν ουν Σωκρατης εργῳ το απορρητον δεικνος, του μυθου ουδεν πλεον προστιθμσι του ως εν τινι φρουρα εσμεν. Ὁι δε εξηγηται τον μυθον προστιθεασιν εξωθεν.

After this he beautifully observes, "That these four govern-ments signify the different gradations of virtues, according to which our soul contains the symbols of all the qualities, both contemplative and purifying, social and ethical; for it either operates according to the theoretic or contemplative virtues, the model of which is the government of Uranus or *Heaven*, that we may begin from on high; and on this account Uranus (*Heaven*) is so called παρα του τα ανω ὁρᾳν, from beholding the things above: Or it lives purely, the exemplar of which is the Kronian or Saturnian kingdom; and on this account Kronos is named as Koro-nous, one who perceives through himself. Hence he is said to devour his own offspring, signifying the conversion of himself into his own substance:—or it operates ac-cording to the social virtues, the symbol of which is the government of Jupiter. Hence, Jupiter is styled the *Demiurgus*, as operating about secondary things:—or it operates according to both the ethical and physical virtues, the symbol of which is the kingdom of Bacchus; and on this account is fabled to be torn in pieces by the Titans, because the virtues are not cut off by each other."

Αινυττονται (lege αινιττονται) δε τους διαφερους βαθμους των αρετων καθ' ας ἡ ἡμετερα ψυχη συμβολα εχουσα πασων των αρετων, των τε θεωρητικων, και καθαρτικων, και πολιτικων, και ηθικων. Ἡ γαρ κατα τας θεωρητικας ενεργει ὡν παρα δειγμα ἡ του ουρανου βασιλεια, ινα ανωθεν αρξαμεθα, διο και ουρανος ειρηται παρα του τα ανω ὁρᾳν.

Ἡ καθαρτικως ζῃ, ἧς παρα δειγμα ἡ Κρονεια βασιλεια, διο και Κρονος ειρηται οιον ὁ κορονους τις ων δια το εαυτον ὁραν. Διο και καταπινειν τα οικεια γεννηματα λεγεται, ως αυτος προς εαυτον επιστεφων. Ἡ κατα τας πολιτικας ὡν συμβολον, ἡ του Διος βασιλεια, διο και δημιουργος ὁ Ζευς, ως περι τα δευτερα ενεργων. Ἡ κατα τας ηθικας και φυσικας αρετας, ὡν συνβολον, ἡ του Διονυσου βασιλεια, διο και σπαραττεται, διοτι ουκ αντακολουθουσιν αλληλαις αἱ αρεται.

And thus far Olympiodorus; in which passages it is necessary to observe, that as the Titans are the artificers of things, and stand next in order to their creations, men are said to be composed from their fragments, because the human soul has a partial life capable of proceeding to the most extreme division united with its proper nature. And while the soul is in a state of servitude to the body, she lives confined, as it were, in bonds, through the dominion of this *Titanical life*. We may observe farther concerning these dramatic shows of the Lesser Mysteries, that as they were intended to represent the condition of the soul while subservient to the body, we shall find that a liberation from this servitude, through the purifying disciplines, potencies that separate from evil, was what the wisdom of the ancients intended to signify by the descent of Hercules, Ulysses, etc., into Hades, and their speedy return from its dark abodes. "Hence," says Proclus, "Hercules being purified by *sacred initiations*, obtained at length a perfect establishment among the gods:" [40] that is, well knowing the dreadful condition of his soul while in captivity to a corporeal nature, and purifying himself by practice of the cleansing virtues, of which certain purifications in the mystic ceremonies were symbolical, he at length was freed from the bondage of matter, and

Eleusinian Mysteries.

ascended beyond her reach. On this account, it is said of him, that

"He dragg'd the three-mouth'd dog to upper day;"

intimating that by temperance, continence, and the other virtues, he drew upwards the intuitional, rational, and opinionative part of the soul. And as to Theseus, who is represented as suffering eternal punishment in Hades, we must consider him too as an allegorical character, of which Proclus, in the above-cited admirable work, gives the following beautiful explanation: "Theseus and Pirithous," says he, "are fabled to have abducted Helen, and descended to the infernal regions, *i. e.* they were lovers both of mental and visible beauty. Afterward one of these (Theseus), on account of his magnanimity, was liberated by Hercules from Hades; but the other (Pirithous) remained there, because he could not attain the difficult height of divine contemplation." This account, indeed, of Theseus can by no means be reconciled with Virgil's:

−sedet, æternumque sedebit,
Infelix Theseus.[*]

Nor do I see how Virgil can be reconciled with himself, who, a little before this, represents him as liberated from Hades. The conjecture, therefore, of Hyginus is most probable, that Virgil in this particular committed an oversight, which, had he lived, he would

---

* "There sits, and forever shall sit, the unhappy Theseus."

doubtless have detected, and amended. This is at least much more probable than the opinion of Dr. Warburton, that Theseus was a living character, who once entered into the Eleusinian Mysteries by force, for which he was imprisoned upon earth, and afterward punished in the infernal realms. For if this was the case, why is not Hercules also represented as in punishment? and this with much greater reason, since he actually dragged Cerberus from Hades; whereas the fabulous descent of Theseus was attended with no real, but only intentional, mischief. Not to mention that Virgil appears to be the only writer of antiquity who condemns this hero to an eternity of pain.

Nor is the secret meaning of the fables concerning the punishment of impure souls less impressive and profound, as the following extract from the manuscript commentary of Olympiodorus on the *Gorgias* of Plato will abundantly affirm:—"Ulysses," says he, "descending into Hades, saw, among others, Sisyphus, and Tityus, and Tantalus. Tityus he saw lying on the earth, and a vulture devouring his liver; the liver signifying that he lived solely according to the principle of cupidity in his nature, and through this was indeed internally prudent; but the earth signifies that his disposition was sordid. But Sisyphus, living under the dominion of ambition and anger, was employed in continually rolling a stone up an eminence, because it perpetually descended again; its descent implying the vicious government of himself; and his rolling the stone, the hard, refractory, and, as it were, rebounding condition of his life. And, lastly, he saw Tantalus extended by the side of a lake, and that there was a tree before him, with abundance of fruit on its branches, which he desired to gather, but it vanished from his view; and this indeed indicates, that he lived under the dominion of phantasy; but his hanging over the lake, and in vain attempting to drink, implies the elusive, humid, and rapidly-gliding condition of such a life." Ὁ Οδυσσευς κατελθων εις ᾁδου, οιδε τον Σισυψον, και τον Τιτυον, και τον Τανταλον. Και τον μεν Τιτυον, επι της γης ειδε κειμενον, και οτι το ἡπαρ αυτου ἡσθιεν γυψ. Το μεν ουν ἡπαρ σημαινει οτι κατα το επιθυμητικον μερος εζησε, και δια τουτο εσω φροντιζετο. Ἡ δε γη σημαινει το χθονιον αυτου φρονημα. Ο δε Σισυφος, κατα το φιλοτιμον, και θυμοειδες ζησας εκυλιε τον λιθον, και παλιν κατεφερεν, επειδε περι αυτα καταρρει, ο κακως πολιτευομενος. Αιθον δε εκυλιε, δια το σκληρον, και αντιτυπον της αυτου ζωης. Τον δε Τανταλον ειδεν εν λιμν (lege λιμνη) και οτι εν δενδροις ησαν οπωραι, και ηθελε τρυγαν, και αφανεις εγινοντο αἱ οπωραι. Τουτο δε σημαινει την κατα φαντασιαν ζωην. Αυτη δε σημανει το ολισθηρον και διυργον, και θαττονα ποπαυομενον. So that according to the wisdom of the ancients, and the most sublime philosophy, the misery which a soul endures in the present life, when giving itself up to the dominion of the irrational part, is nothing more than the commencement, as it were, of that torment which it win experience hereafter: a torment the same in kind though different in degree, as it will be much more dreadful, vehement, and extended. And by the above specimen, the reader may perceive how infinitely superior the explanation which the Platonic philosophy affords of these fables is to the frigid and trifling interpretations of Bacon and other modern mythologists; who are able indeed to point out their correspondence to something in the natural or moral world, because such is the wonderful connection of things, that all things sympathize with all, but are at the same time ignorant that these fables were composed by men divinely wise, who framed them after the model of the highest originals, from the contemplation of *real and permanent being*, and not from regarding the delusive and fluctuating objects of sense. This, indeed, will be evident to every ingenuous mind, from reflecting that these wise men universally considered Hell or death as commencing in the present life (as we have already abundantly proved), and that, consequently, sense is nothing more than the energy of the dormant soul, and a perception, as it were, of the delusions of dreams. In consequence of this, it is absurd in the highest degree to imagine that such men would compose fables from the contemplation of shadows only, without regarding the splendid originals from which these dark phantoms were produced:—not to mention that their harmonizing so much more perfectly with intellectual explications is an indisputable proof that they were derived from an intellectual [noetic] source.

Torch-bearer as Apollo. Faun and Bacchante.

And thus much for the dramatic shows of the Lesser Mysteries, or the first part of these sacred institutions, which was properly denominated τελετη [*telete*, the closing up] and μυησις *muesis* [the initiation], as containing certain perfective rites, symbolical exhibitions and the imparting and reception of sacred doctrines, previous to the beholding of the most splendid visions, or εποπτεια [*epopteia*, seership]. For thus the gradation of the Mysteries is disposed by Proclus in *Theology of Plato*, book iv. "The perfective rite [τελετη, *telete*]," says he, "precedes in order the *initiation* [μυησις, *muesis*], and *initiation*, the final apocalypse, *epopteia*." Προηγειται γαρ, ή μεν τελετη της μυσεως, αυτη δε της εποπτειας. [41] At the same time it is proper to observe that the whole business of initiation was distributed into five parts, as we are informed by Theon of Smyrna, in *Mathematica*, who thus elegantly compares philosophy to these mystic rites: "Again," says he, "philosophy may be called the initiation into true sacred ceremonies, and the instruction in genuine Mysteries; for there are five parts of initiation: the first of which is the previous purification; for neither are the Mysteries communicated to all who are willing to receive them; but there are certain persons who are prevented by the voice of the crier [κηρυξ, *kerux*], such as those who possess impure hands and an inarticulate voice; since it is necessary that such as are not expelled from the Mysteries should first be refined by certain purifications: but after purification, the reception of the sacred rites succeeds. The third part is denominated *epopteia*, or reception. [42] And the fourth, which is the end and design of the revelation, is [the investiture] the binding of the head and fixing of the crowns. The initiated person is, by this means, authorized to communicate to others the sacred rites in which he has been instructed; whether after this he becomes a torch-bearer, or an hierophant of the Mysteries, or sustains some other part of the sacerdotal office. But the fifth, which is produced from all these, is *friendship and interior communion with God*, and the enjoyment of that felicity which arises from intimate converse with divine beings. Similar to this is the communication of political instruction; for, in the first place, a certain purification precedes, or else an exercise in proper mathematical discipline from early youth. For thus Empedocles asserts, that it is necessary to be purified from sordid concerns, by drawing from five fountains, with a vessel of indissoluble brass: but Plato, that purification is to be derived from the five mathematical disciplines, namely from arithmetic, geometry, stereometry, music, and astronomy; but the philosophical instruction in theorems, logical, political, and physical, is similar to initiation. But he (that is, Plato) denominates εποπτεια [or the revealing], a contemplation of things which are apprehended intuitively, absolute truths, and ideas. But he considers the binding of the head, and coronation, as analogous to the authority which any one receives from his instructors, of leading others to the same contemplation. And the fifth gradation is, the most perfect felicity arising from hence, and, according to Plato, *an assimilation to divinity*, as far as is possible to mankind." But though εποπτεια, or the rendition of the arcane ideas, principally characterized the Greater Mysteries, yet this was likewise accompanied with the μυησις, or initiation, as will be evident in the course of this inquiry.

But let us now proceed to the doctrine of the Greater Mysteries: and here I shall endeavor to prove that as the dramatic shows of the Lesser Mysteries occultly signified the miseries of the soul while in subjection to body, so those of the Greater obscurely intimated, by mystic and splendid visions, the felicity of the soul both here and hereafter, when purified from the defilements of a material nature, and constantly elevated to the realities of intellectual [spiritual] vision. Hence, as the ultimate design of the Mysteries, according to Plato, was to lead us back to the principles from which we descended, that is, to a perfect enjoyment of intellectual [spiritual] good, the imparting of these principles was doubtless one part of the doctrine contained in the απορρητα, *aporrheta,* or secret discourses; [43] and the different purifications exhibited in these rites, in conjunction with initiation and the *epopteia* were symbols of the gradation of virtues requisite to this reascent of the soul. And hence, too, if this be the case, a representation of the descent of the soul [from its former heavenly estate] must certainly form no inconsiderable part of these mystic shows; all which the following observations will, I do not doubt, abundantly evince.

In the first place, then, that the shows of the Greater Mysteries occultly signified the felicity of the soul both here and hereafter, when separated from the contact and influence of the body, is evident from what has been demonstrated in the former part of this discourse: for if *he who in the present life is in subjection to his irrational part is truly in Hades, he who is superior to its dominion is likewise an inhabitant of a place totally different from Hades.* [44]

If Hades therefore is the region or condition of punishment and misery, the purified soul must reside in the regions of bliss; in a life and condition of purity and contemplation in the present life, and entheastically, [45] animated by the divine energy, in the next. This being admitted, let us proceed to consider the description which Virgil gives us of these fortunate abodes, and the latent signification which it contains. Æneas and his guide, then, having passed through Hades, and seen at a distance Tartarus, or the utmost profundity of a material nature, they next advance to the Elysian fields:

Devenere locus lætos, et amæna vireta
Fortunatorum nemorum, sedesque beatas.
Largior hic campos æther et lumine vestit
Purpureo; solemque suum, sua sidera norunt.[*]

Now the secret meaning of these joyful places is thus beautifully unfolded by Olympiodorus in his manuscript Commentary on the *Gorgias* of Plato. "It is necessary to know," says he, "that the *fortunate islands* are said to be raised above the sea; and hence a condition of being, which transcends this corporeal life and generated existence, is denominated the islands of the blessed; but these are the same with the Elysian fields. And on this account Hercules is said to have accomplished his last labor in the Hesperian regions; signifying by this, that having vanquished a dark and earthly life he afterward lived in day, that is, in truth and light." Δει δε ειδεναι

---

* "They came to the blissful regions, and delightful green retreats, and happy abodes in the fortunate groves. A freer and purer sky here clothes the fields with a purple light; they recognize their own sun, their own stars."

ότι αἱ νησοι ὑπερκυπτουσιν της θαλασσης ανωτερω ουσαι. Την ουν πολιτειαν την ὑπερκυψασαν του βιου και της γενησεως, μακαρων νησους καλουσι. Ταυτον δε εστι και το ηλυσιον πεδιον. Δια τοι τουτο και ὁ Ἡρακλης τελευταιον αθλον εν τοις εσπεριοις μερεσιν εποιησατο, αντι κατηγωνισατο τον σκοτεινον και χθονιον βιον, και λοιπον εν ἡμερᾳ, ὁστιν εν αληθειᾳ και φωτι εζη. So that he who in the present state vanquishes as much as possible a corporeal life, through the practice of the purifying virtues, passes in reality into the Fortunate Islands of the soul, and lives surrounded with the bright splendors of truth and wisdom proceeding from the sun of good.

The poet, in describing the employments of the blessed, says:

Pars in gramineis exercent membra palæstris:
Contendunt ludo, et fulva luctantur arena:
Pars pedibus plaudunt choreas, et carmina dicunt.
Nec non Threicius longa cum veste sacerdos
Obloquitur numeris septem discrimina vocum:
Iamque eadem digitis, jam pectine pulsat eburno.
Hic genus antiquum Teueri, pulcherrima proles,
Magnanimi heroes, nati melioribus annis,
Illusque, Assaracusque, et Trojæ Dardanus auctor.
Arma procul, currusque virum miratur inanis.
Stant terra defixæ hastæ, passimque soluti
Per campum pascuntur equi. Quæ gratia curruum
Armorumque fuit vivis, quæ cura nitentis
Pascere equos, eadem sequitur tellure repostos.
Conspicit, ecce alios, dextra lævaque per herbam

Vescentis, lætumque choro Pæana canentis,
Inter odoratum lauri nemus: unde superne
Plurimus Eridani per silvam volvitur amnis.[*]

A pæon was chanted to Apollo at Delphi every seventh day. This must not be understood as if the soul in the regions of felicity retained any affection for material concerns, or was engaged in the trifling pursuits of the everyday corporeal life; but that when separated from generation, and the world's life, she is constantly engaged in employments proper to the higher spiritual nature; either in divine contests of the most exalted wisdom; in forming the responsive dance of refined imaginations; in tuning the sacred lyre of mystic piety to strains of divine fury and ineffable delight; in giving free scope to the splendid and winged powers of the soul; or in nourishing the higher intellect with the substantial banquets of intelligible [spiritual] food. Nor is it without reason that the river Eridanus is represented as flowing through these delightful abodes; and is at the same time denominated *plurimus* (greatest), because a great part of it was absorbed in the earth without emerging from

---

* "Some exercise their limbs upon the grassy field, contend in play and wrestle on the yellow sand; some dance on the ground and utter songs. The priestly Thracian, likew se, in his long robe [Orpheus] responds in melodious numbers to the seven distinguished notes; and now strikes them with his fingers, now with the ivory quill. Here are also the ancient race of Teucer, a most illustrious progeny, noble heroes, born in happier years,—Il, Assarac, and Dardan, the founder of Troy. Æneas looking from afar, admires the arms and empty war-cars of the heroes. There stood spears fixed in the ground, and scattered over the plain horses are feeding. The same taste which when alive p. 95 these men had for chariots and arms, the same passion for rearing glossy steeds, follow them reposing beneath the earth. Lo! also he views others, on the right and left, feasting on the grass, and singing in chorus the joyful pæon, amid a fragrant grove of laurel; whence from above the greatest river Eridanus rolls through the woods."

Eleusinian Mysteries.

thence: for a river is the symbol of life, and consequently signifies in this place the *intellectual or spiritual life, proceeding from on high,* that is, from divinity itself, and gliding with prolific energy through the hidden and profound recesses of the soul.

In the following lines he says:

Nulli certa domus. Lucis habitamus opacis,
Riparumque toros, et prata recentia rivis
Incolimus.[*]

By the blessed not being confined to a particular habitation, is implied that they are perfectly free in all things; being entirely free from all material restraint, and purified from all inclination incident to the dark and cold tenement of the body. The shady groves are symbols of the retiring of the soul to the depth of her essence, and there, by energy solely divine, establishing herself in the ineffable principle of things. [46] And the meadows are symbols of that prolific power of the gods through which all the variety of reasons, animals, and forms was produced, and which is here the refreshing pasture and retreat of the liberated soul.

But that the communication of the knowledge of the principles from which the soul descended formed a part of the sacred Mysteries is evident from Virgil; and that this was accompanied with a vision of these principles or gods, is no less certain, from

---

* "No one of us has a fixed abode. We inhabit the dark groves, and occupy couches on the river-banks, and meadows fresh with little rivulets."

the testimony of Plato, Apuleius, and Proclus. The first part of this assertion is evinced by the following beautiful lines:

Principio cælum ac terras, camposque liquentes
Lucentemque globum lunæ, Titaniaque astra
Spiritus intus alit, totumque infusa per artus
Mens agitat molem, et magno se corpore miscet.
Inde hominum pecudumque genus, vitæque volantum,
Et quæ marmoreo fert monstra sub æquore pontus.
Igneus est ollis vigor, et cælestis origo
Seminibus, quantum non noxia corpora tardant,
Terrenique hebetant artus, moribundaque membra.
Hinc metuunt cupiuntque: dolent, gaudentque: neque auras
Despiciunt clausa tenebris et carcere cæco.[*]

For the sources of the soul's existence are also the principles from which it fell; and these, as we may learn from the *Timæus* of Plato, are the Demiurgus, the mundane soul, and the junior or mundane gods. [47] Now, of these, the mundane intellect, which, according to the ancient theology, is represented by Bacchus, is principally celebrated by the poet, and this because the soul is particularly dis-

---

* "First of all the interior spirit sustains the heaven and earth and watery plains, the illuminated orb of the moon, and the Titanian stars; and the Mind, diffused through all the members, gives energy to the whole frame, and mingles with the vast body [of the universe]. Thence proceed the race of men and beasts, the vital souls of birds and the brutes which the Ocean breeds beneath its smooth surface. In them all is a potency like fire, and a celestial origin as to the rudimentary principles, so far as they are not clogged by noxious bodies. They are deadened by earthly forms and members subject to death; hence they fear and desire, grieve and rejoice; nor do they, thus enclosed in darkness and the gloomy prison, behold the heavenly air."

tributed into generation, after the manner of Dionysus or Bacchus, as is evident from the preceding extracts from Olympiodorus: and is still more abundantly confirmed by the following curious passage from the same author, in his comment on the *Phædo* of Plato. "The soul," says he, "descends Corically [or after the manner of Proserpine] into generation, [48] but is distributed into generation Dionysiacally, [49] and she is bound in body Prometheiacally [50] and Titanically: she frees herself therefore from its bonds by exercising the strength of Hercules; but she is collected into one through the assistance of Apollo and the savior Minerva, by philosophical discipline of mind and heart purifying the nature." Ὅτι κορικως μεν εις γενεσιν κατεισιν ἡ ψυχη· Διονυσιανως δε μεριζεται ὑπο της γενεσεως· Προμηθειως δε, και Τιτανικως, εγκαταδειται τω σωματι· Αυει μεν ουν εαυτην Ἡρακλειως ισχυσασα· Συναιρει δε δι Απολλωνος και της σωτηρας Αθηνας, παθαρτικως τω οντι φιλοσοφουσα. The poet, however, intimates the other causes of the soul's existence, when he says,

Igneus est ollis vigor, *et cælestis origo*
Seminibus– [*]

which evidently alludes to the *sowing* of souls into generation, [51] mentioned in the *Timæus*. And from hence the reader will easily perceive the extreme ridiculousness of Dr. Warburton's system, that the grand secret of the Mysteries consisted in exposing the errors of Polytheism, and in teaching the doctrine of the unity, or the

---

* "There is then a certain fiery potency, and a celestial origin as to the rudimentary principles." I. e. Restored to wholeness and divine life.

existence of one deity alone. For he might as well have said, that the great secret consisted in teaching a man how, by writing notes on the works of a poet, he might become a *bishop!* But it is by no means wonderful that men who have not the smallest conception of the true nature of the gods; who have persuaded themselves that they were only dead men deified; and who measure the understandings of the ancients by their own, should be led to fabricate a system so improbable and absurd.

But that this instruction was accompanied with a vision of the source from which the soul proceeded, is evident from the express testimony, in the first place, of Apuleius, who thus describes his initiation into the Mysteries. "Accessi confinium mortis; et calcato Proserpinæ limine, per omnia vectus elementa remeavi. Nocte media vidi solem candido coruscantem lumine, *deos inferos, et deos super-os.* Accessi coram, et adoravi de proximo." [52] That is, "I approached the confines of death: and having trodden on the threshold of Proserpina returned, having been carried through all the elements. In the depths of midnight I saw the sun glittering with a splendid light, *together with the infernal and supernal gods:* and to these divinities approaching near, I paid the tribute of devout adoration." And this is no less evidently implied by Plato, who thus describes the felicity of the holy soul prior to its descent, in a beautiful allusion to the arcane visions of the Mysteries. Καλλος δε τοτε ην ιδειν λαμπρον, ότε συν ευδαιμονι χορῳ μακαριαν οψιν τε και θεαν επομενοι μετα μεν Διος ήμεις, αλλοι δε μετ' αλλου θεων, ειδον τε και ετελουντο τελετων ήν θεμις λεγειν μακαριωτατην· ην οργιαζομεν ολοκληροι μεν αυτοι οντες, και απαθεις κακων όσα ήμας εν ύστερω χρονω ύπεμενεν. Όλοκληρα δε και άπλα και ατρεμη και ευδαιμονα φασματα μυουμενοι τε και εποπτευοντες εν αυγη καθαρα, καθαροι οντες και ασημαντοι τουτου ό νυν δη σωμα περιφεροντες ονομαζομεν οστρεου τροπον δε δεσμευμενοι. That is, "But it was then lawful to survey the most splendid beauty, when we obtained, together with that blessed choir, this happy vision and contemplation. And we indeed enjoyed this blessed spectacle together with Jupiter; but others in conjunction with some other god; at the same time being *initiated* in those *Mysteries*, which it is lawful to call the most blessed of all Mysteries. And these divine *Orgies* [53] were celebrated by us, while we possessed the proper integrity of our nature, we were freed from the molestations of evil which otherwise await us in a future period of time. Likewise, in consequence of this divine *initiation*, we became *spectators* of entire, simple, immovable, and *blessed visions*, resident in a pure light; and were ourselves pure and immaculate, being liberated from this surrounding vestment, which we denominate body, and to which we are now bound like an oyster to its shell." [54] Upon this beautiful passage Proclus observes, "That the *initiation* and *epopteia* [the vailing and the revealing] are symbols of ineffable silence, and of union with mystical natures, through intelligible visions. [55] Και γαρ ή μυησις, και η εποπτεια, της αρρήτου σιγης εστι συμβολον, και της προς τα μυστικα διὰ των νοητων φασματων ενωσεως. Now, from all this, it may be inferred, that the most sublime part of the εποπτιεια [*epopteia*] or final revealing, consisted in beholding the gods themselves invested with a resplendent light; [56] and that this was symbolical of those transporting visions, which the virtuous soul will constantly enjoy in a future state; and of which it is able to gain some ravishing glimpses, even while connected with the cumbrous vestment of the body. [57]

But that this was actually the case, is evident from the following unequivocal testimony of Proclus: Εν απασι ταις τελεταις και τοις μυστηριοις, οἱ θεοι πολλας μεν εαυτων προτεινουσι μορφας, πολλα δε σχηματα εξαλαττοντες φαινονται· και τοτε μεν ατυπωτον αυτων προβεβληται φως, τοτε δε εις ανθρωπειον μορφην εσχηματισμενον, τοτε δε εις ἀλλοιον τυπον προεληλυθως. *l. e.* "In all the initiations and Mysteries, the gods exhibit many forms of themselves, and appear in a variety of shapes: and sometimes, indeed, a formless light [58] of themselves is held forth to the view; sometimes this light is according to a human form, and sometimes it proceeds into a different shape." [59] This assertion of divine visions in the Mysteries, is clearly confirmed by Plotinus. [60] And, in short, that magical evocation formed a part of the sacerdotal office in the Mysteries, and that this was universally believed by all antiquity, long before the era of the latter Platonists, [61] is plain from the testimony of Hippocrates, or at least Democritus, in his Treatise *de Morbo Sacro*. [62] For speaking of those who attempt to cure this disease by magic, he observes: ει γαρ σεληνην τε καθαιρειν, και ἡλιον αφανιζειν, χειμωνα τε και ευδιην ποιειν, και ομβρους και αυχμους, και θαλασσαν αφορον και γην, και τ'αλλα τα τοιουτοτροπα παντα επιδεχονται επιστασθαι, ειτε και εκ ΤΕΛΕΤΩΝ, ειτε και εξ αλλης τινος γνωμης μελετης φασιν οιοι τε ειναι οι ταυτα επιτηδευοντες δυσεβεειν εμοι γε δοκεουσι. κ. λ. *l. e.* "For if they profess themselves able to draw down the moon, to obscure the sun, to produce stormy and pleasant weather, as likewise showers

Eleusinian Mysteries. Etruscan.

of rain, and heats, and to render the sea and earth barren, and to accomplish every thing else of this kind; whether they derive this knowledge from *the Mysteries*, or from some other mental effort or meditation, they appear to me to be impious, from the study of such concerns." From all which is easy to see, how egregiously Dr. Warburton was mistaken, when, in page 231 of his *Divine Legation*, he asserts, "that the light beheld in the Mysteries, was nothing more than an illuminated image which the priests had thoroughly purified."

But he is likewise no less mistaken, in transferring the injunction given in one of the *Magic Oracles* of Zoroaster, to the business of the Eleusinian Mysteries, and in perverting the meaning of the Oracle's admonition. For thus the Oracle speaks:

Μη φυσεως καλεσης αυτοπτον αγαλμα,
Ου γαρ χρη κεινους σε βλεπειν πριν σωμα τελεσθη.

Satyr, Cupid, and Venus.

Cupids, Satyr, and statue of Priapus.

That is, "Invoke not the *self-revealing image of Nature*, for you must not behold these things before your body has received the initiation." Upon which he observes, *"that the self-revealing image was only a diffusive shining light, as the name partly declares."* [63] But this is a piece of gross ignorance, from which he might have been freed by an attentive perusal of Proclus on the *Timæus* of Plato: for in these truly divine Commentaries we learn, "that the moon [64] is the cause of nature to mortals, *and the self-revealing image of the fountain of nature.*" Σεληνη μεν αιτια τοις θνητοις της φυσεως, το αυτοπτον αγαλμα ουσα της πηγαιας φυσεως. If the reader is desirous of knowing what we are to understand by the fountain of nature of which the moon is the image, let him attend to the following information, derived from a long and deep study of the ancient theology: for from hence I have learned, that there are many divine fountains contained in the essence of the demiurgus of the world; and that among these there are three of a very distinguished rank, namely, the fountain of souls, or Juno,—the fountain of virtues, or Minerva—and the fountain of nature, or Diana. This last fountain too immediately depends on the vivifying goddess Rhea; and was assumed by the Demiurgus among the rest, as necessary to the prolific reproduction of himself. And this information will enable us besides to explain the meaning of the following passages in Apuleius, which, from not being understood, have induced the moderns to believe that Apuleius acknowledged but one deity alone. The first of these passages is in the beginning of the eleventh book of his *Metamorphoses*, in which the divinity of the moon is represented as addressing him in this sublime manner: "En adsum tuis commota, Luci, precibus, rerum Natura parens, elementorum omnium domina, seculorum progenies initialis, summa numinum, regina Manium, prima cælitum, Deorum Dearumque facies uniformis: quæ cæli luminosa culmina, maris salubria flamina, inferorum de plorata silentia nutibus meis dispenso: cujus numen unicum, multiformi specie, ritu vario, nomine multijugo totus veneratur orbis. Me primigenii Phryges Pessinunticam nominant Deûm matrem. Hinc Autochthones Attici Cecropiam Minervam; illinc fluctuantes Cyprii Paphiam Venerem: Cretes sagittiferi Dictynnam Dianam; Siculi trilingues Stygiam Proserpinam; Eleusinii vetustam Deam Cererem: Junonem alii, alii Bellonam, alii Hecaten, Rhamnusiam alii. Et qui nascentis dei Solis inchoantibus radiis illustrantur, Æthiopes, Ariique, priscaque doctrina pollentes Ægyptii cærimoniis me prorsus propriis percolentes appellant vero nomine reginam Isidem." That is, "Behold, Lucius, moved with thy supplications, I am present; I, who am *Nature*, the parent of things, mistress of all the elements, initial progeny of the ages, the highest of the divinities, queen of departed spirits, the first of the celestials, of gods and goddesses the sole likeness of all: who rule by my nod the luminous heights of the heavens, the salubrious breezes of the sea, and the woful silences of the infernal regions, and whose divinity, in itself but one, is venerated by all the earth, in many characters, various rites, and different appellations. Hence the primitive Phrygians call me Pessinuntica, the mother of the gods; the Attic Autochthons, Cecropian Minerva; the wave-surrounded Cyprians, Paphian Venus; the arrow-bearing Cretans, Dictynnian Diana; the three-tongued Sicilians, Stygian Proserpina; and the inhabitants of Eleusis, the ancient goddess Ceres. Some, again, have invoked me as Juno, others as Bellona, others as Hecaté, and others as Rhamnusia; and those who are enlightened by the emerging rays of the rising sun, the Æthiopians, and Aryans, and likewise the Ægyptians powerful in ancient learning, who reverence my divinity with ceremonies perfectly proper, call me by my true appellation Queen Isis." And, again, in another place of the same book, he says of the moon: "Te Superi colunt, observant Inferi: tu rotas orbem, luminas Solem, regis mundum, calcas Tartarum. Tibi respondent sidera, gaudent numina, redeunt tempora, serviunt elementa, etc." That is, "The supernal gods reverence thee, and those in the realms beneath attentively do homage to thy divinity. Thou dost make the universe revolve, illuminate the sun, govern the world, and tread on Tartarus. The stars answer thee, the gods rejoice, the hours and seasons return by thy appointment, and the elements serve thee." For all this easily follows, if we consider it as addressed to the fountain-deity of nature, subsisting in the Demiurgus, and which is the exemplar of that nature which flourishes in the lunar orb, and throughout the material world, and from which the deity itself of the moon originally proceeds. Hence, as this fountain immediately depends on the life-giving goddess Rhea, the reason is obvious, why it was formerly worshiped as the mother of the gods: and as all the mundane are contained in the super-mundane gods, the other appellations are to be considered as names of the several mundane divinities produced by this fountain, and in whose essence they are likewise contained.

Diana and Endymion. Apollo and Daphne.

But to proceed with our inquiry, I shall, in the next place, prove that the different purifications exhibited in these rites, in conjunction with initiation and the epopteia were symbols of the gradation of disciplines requisite to the reascent of the soul. [65] And the first part, indeed, of this proposition respecting the purifications, immediately follows from the testimony of Plato in the passage already adduced, in which he asserts that the ultimate design of the Mysteries was to lead us back to the principles from which we originally fell. For if the Mysteries were symbolical, as is universally acknowledged, this must likewise be true of the purifications as a part of the Mysteries; and as inward purity, of which the external is symbolical, can only be obtained by the exercise of the virtues, it evidently follows that the purifications were symbols of the purifying moral virtues. And the latter part of the proposition may be easily inferred, from the passage already cited from the *Phædrus* of Plato, in which he compares *initiation* and the *epopteia* to the blessed vision of the higher intelligible natures; an employment which can alone belong to the exercise of contemplation. But the whole of this is rendered indisputable by the following remarkable testimony of Olympiodorus, in his excellent manuscript Commentary on the *Phædo* of Plato. [66] "In the sacred rites," says he, "popular purifications are in the first place brought forth, and after these such as are more arcane. But, in the third place, collections of various things into one are received; after which follows inspection. The ethical and political virtues therefore are analogous to the apparent purifications; the cathartic virtues which banish all external impressions, correspond to the more arcane purifications. The theoretical energies about intelligibles, are analogous to the collections; and the contraction of these energies into an indivisible nature, corresponds to initiation. And the simple self-inspection of simple forms, is analogous to epoptic vision." Ὅτι εν τοις ἱεροις ἡγουντο μεν αἱ πανδημοι καθαρσεις. Ειτα επι ταυταις απορρητοτεραι·

μετα δε ταυτας συστασεις παρελαμβανοντο, και επι ταυταις μυησεις·
εν τελει δε εποπτειαι. Αναλογουσι τοινυν αἱ μεν ηθικαι και πολιτικαι
αρεται, τοις εμφανεσι καθαρμοις. Αἱ δε καθαρτικαι ὁσαι αποσκευαζονται
παντα τα ἑκτος τοις απορρητοτεροις. Αἱ δε περι τα νοητα θεωρητικαι τε
ενεργειαι ταις συστασεσιν. Αἱ δε τουτων συναιρεσεις εις το αμεριστον
ταις μυησεσιν. Αἱ δε ἁπλαι των ἁπλων ειδων αυτοψιαι ταις εποπτειαις.
And here I can not refrain from noticing, with indignation mingled
with pity, the ignorance and arrogance of modern critics, who pre-
tend that this distribution of the virtues is entirely the invention of
the latter Platonists, and without any foundation in the writings of
Plato. [67] And among the supporters of such ignorance, I am sorry to
find Fabricius, in his *prolegomena* to the life of Proclus. For nothing
can be more obvious to every reader of Plato than that in his *Laws*
he treats of the social and political virtues; in his *Phædo*, and seventh
book of the *Republic*, of the purifying; and in his *Thæatetus*, of the
contemplative and sublimer virtues. This observation is, indeed, so
obvious, in the *Phædo*, with respect to the purifying virtues, that no
one but a verbal critic could read this dialogue and be insensible to
its truth: for Socrates in the very beginning expressly asserts that it
is the business of philosophers to study to die, and to be themselves
dead, [68] and yet at the same time reprobates suicide. What then can
such a death mean but symbolical or philosophical death? And what
is this but the true exercise of the virtues which purify? But these
poor men read only superficially, or for the sake of displaying some
critical *acumen* in verbal emendations; and yet with such despicable
preparations for philosophical discussion, they have the impudence
to oppose their puerile conceptions to the decisions of men of ele-

vated genius and profound investigation, who, happily freed from the danger and drudgery of learning any foreign language, [69] directed all their attention without restraint to the acquisition of the most exalted truth.

It only now remains that we prove, in the last place, that a representation of the descent of the soul formed no inconsiderable part of these mystic shows. This, indeed, is doubtless occultly intimated by Virgil, when speaking of the souls of the blessed in Elysium, he adds,

Has omnes, ubi mille rotam volvere per annos,
Lethaeum ad fluvium deus evocat agmine magno:
Scilicet immemores supera ut convexa revisant,
Rursus et incipiant in corpore velle reverti.[*]

But openly by Apuleius in the following prayer which Psyché addresses to Ceres: Per ego te frugiferam tuam dextram istam deprecor, per lætificas messium cærimonias, per tacita sacra cistarum, et per famulorum tuorum draconum pinnata curricula, et glebæ. Siculæ fulcamina, et currum rapacem, et terram tenacem, et illuminarum Proserpinæ nuptiarum demeacula, et cætera quæ silentio tegit Eleusis, Atticæ sacrarium; miserandæ Psyches animæ, supplicis tuæ, subsiste. [70] That is, "I beseech thee, by thy fruit-bearing right hand, by the joyful ceremonies of harvest, by the occult sacred rites of thy cistæ, [71] and by the winged car of thy attending dragons, and

---

* "All these, after they have passed away a thousand years, are summoned by the divine one in great array, to the Lethæan river. In this way they become forgetful of their former earth-life, and revisit the vaulted realms of the world, willing again to return into bodies."

the furrows of the Sicilian soil, and the rapacious chariot (or car of the ravisher), *and the dark descending ceremonies attending the marriage of Proserpina, and the ascending rites which accompanied the lighted return of thy daughter, and by other arcana which Eleusis the Attic sanctuary conceals in profound silence*, relieve the sorrows of thy wretched suppliant Psyché." For the abduction of Proserpina signifies the descent of the soul, as is evident from the passage previously adduced from Olympiodorus, in which he says the soul descends Corically; [72] and this is confirmed by the authority of the philosopher Sallust, who observes, "That the abduction of Proserpina is fabled to have taken place about the opposite equinoctial; and by this the descent of souls [into earth-life] is implied." Περι γουν την εναντιαν ισημεριαν ἡ της Κορης ἁρπαγη μυθολογειται γενεσθαι, ὁ δη καθοδος εστι των ψυχων. [73] And as the abduction of Proserpina was exhibited in the dramatic representations of the Mysteries, as is clear from Apuleius, it indisputably follows, that this represented the descent of the soul, and its union with the dark tenement of the body. Indeed, if the ascent and descent of the soul, and its condition while connected with a material nature, were represented in the dramatic shows of the Mysteries, it is evident that this was implied by the rape of Proserpina. And the former part of this assertion is manifest from Apuleius, when describing his initiation, he says, in the passage already adduced: "I approached the confines of death, and having trodden on the threshold of Proserpina, *I returned, having been carried through all the elements*." And as to the latter part, it has been amply proved, from the highest authority, in the first division of this discourse.

Nor must the reader be disturbed on finding that, according to Porphyry, as cited by Eusebius, [74] the fable of Proserpina alludes to seed placed in the ground; for this is likewise true of the fable, considered according to its material explanation. But it will be proper on this occasion to rise a little higher, and consider the various species of fables, according to their philosophical arrangement; since by this means the present subject will receive an additional elucidation, and the wisdom of the ancient authors of fables will be vindicated from the unjust aspersions of ignorant declaimers. I shall present the reader, therefore, with the following interesting division of fables,

Ceres lends her ear to Triptolemus.

from the elegant book of the Platonic philosopher Sallust, on the gods and the universe. "Of fables," says he, "some are theological, others physical, others animastic (or relating to soul), others material, and lastly, others mixed from these. Fables are theological which relate to nothing corporeal, but contemplate the very essences of the gods; such as the fable which asserts that Saturn devoured his children: for it insinuates nothing more than the nature of an intellectual (or intuitional) god; since every such intellect returns into itself. We regard fables physically when we speak concerning the operations of the gods about the world; as when considering Saturn the same as Time, and calling the parts of time the children of the universe, we assert that the children are devoured by their parent. But we utter fables in a spiritual mode, when we contemplate the operations of the soul; because the intellections of our souls, though by a discursive energy they go forth into other things, yet abide in their parents. Lastly, fables are material, such as the Egyptians ignorantly employ, considering and calling corporeal natures divinities: such as Isis, earth, Osiris, humidity, Typhon, heat or, again, denominating Saturn water, Adonis, fruits, and Bacchus, wine. And, indeed, to assert that these are dedicated to the gods, in the same manner as herbs, stones, and animals, is the part of wise men; but to call them gods is alone the province of fools and madmen; unless we speak in the same manner as when, from established custom, we call the orb of the sun and its rays the sun itself. But we may perceive the mixed kind of fables, as well in many other particulars, as when they relate that Discord, at a banquet of the gods, threw a golden apple, and that a dispute about it arising among the goddesses, they were sent by Jupiter to take the judgment of Paris, who, charmed with the beauty of Venus, gave her the apple in preference to the rest. For in this fable the banquet denotes the super-mundane powers of the gods; and on this account they subsist in conjunction with each other: but the golden apple denotes the world, which, on account of its composition from contrary natures, is not improperly said to be thrown by Discord, or strife. But again, since different gifts are imparted to the world by different gods, they appear to contest with each other for the apple. And a soul living according to sense (for this is Paris), not perceiving other powers in the universe, asserts that the apple is alone the beauty of Venus.

Proserpina and Pluto. Jupiter angry.

But of these species of fables, such as are theological belong to philosophers; the physical and spiritual to poets; *but the mixed to the first of the initiatory rites* (τελεταῖς); *since the intention of all mystic ceremonies is to conjoin us with the world and the gods."*

Thus far the excellent Sallust: from whence it is evident, that the fable of Proserpina, as belonging to the Mysteries, is properly of a mixed nature, or composed from all the four species of fables, the theological [spiritual or psychical], and material. But in order to understand this divine fable, it is requisite to know, that according to

Proserpina.—Greek. Bacchus.—India.

Ceres.—Roman. Demeter.—Etruscan.

the arcana of the ancient theology, the Coric [75] order (or the order belonging to Proserpina) is twofold, one part of which is super-mundane, subsisting with Jupiter, or the Demiurgus, and thus associated with him establishing one artificer of divisible natures; but the other is mundane, in which Proserpina is said to be ravished by Pluto, and to animate the extremities of the universe. "Hence," says Proclus, "according to the statement of theologists, who delivered to us the most holy Mysteries, she [Proserpina] abides on high in those dwellings of her mother which she prepared for her in inaccessible places, exempt from the sensible world. But she likewise dwells beneath with Pluto, administering terrestrial concerns, governing the recesses of the earth, supplying life to the extremities of the universe, and imparting soul to beings which are rendered by her inanimate and dead." Και γαρ ή των θεολογων φημη, των τας άγιωτατας ήμιν εν Ελευσινι τελετας παραδεδωκοτων, ανω, μεν αυτην εν τοις μητρος οικοις μενειν φησιν, ους ἡ μητηρ αυτη κατεσκεναζεν εν αβατοις εξηρημενους του παντος. Κατω δε μετα Πλουτωνος των χθονιων επαρχειν, και τους της γης μυχους επιτροπευειν, και ζωην επορεγειν τοις εχατοις του παντος, και ψυχης μεταδιδοναι τοις παρ εαυτων αψυχοις και νεχροις. [76] Hence we may easily perceive that this fable is of the mixed kind, one part of which relates to the super-mundane establishment of the secondary cause of life, [77] and the other to the procession or outgoing of life and soul to the farthest extremity of things. Let us therefore more attentively consider the fable, in that part of it which is symbolical of the descent of souls; in order to which, it will be requisite to premise an abridgment of the arcane discourse, respecting the wanderings of Ceres, as preserved by Minutius Felix. "Proserpina," says he, "the daughter of Ceres by Jupiter, as she was gathering tender flowers, in the new spring, was ravished from her delightful abodes by Pluto; and being carried from thence through thick woods, and over a length of sea, was brought by Pluto into a cavern, the residence of departed spirits, over whom she afterward ruled with absolute sway. But Ceres, upon discovering the loss of her daughter, with lighted torches, and begirt with a serpent, wandered over the whole earth for the purpose of finding her till she came to Eleusis; there she found her daughter, and also taught to the Eleusinians the cultivation of corn." Now in this fable *Ceres* represents the evolution of that intuitional part of our nature which we properly denominate *intellect* [78] (or the unfolding of the intuitional faculty of the mind from its quiet and collected condition in the world of thought); and *Proserpina* that living, self-moving, and animating part which we call *soul*. But lest this comparing of unfolded intellect to Ceres should seem ridiculous to the reader, unacquainted with the Orphic theology, it is necessary to inform him that this goddess, from her intimate union with Rhea, in conjunction with whom she produced Jupiter, is evidently of a Saturnian and zoogonic, or intellectual and vivific rank; and hence, as we are informed by the philosopher Sallust, among the mundane divinities she is the deity of the planet Saturn. [79] So that in consequence of this, our intellect (or intuitive faculty) in a descending state must aptly symbolize with the divinity of Ceres. But Pluto signifies the whole of a material nature; since the empire of this god, according to Pythagoras, commences downward from the Galaxy or milky way. And the cavern signifies the entrance, as it were, into the profundities of such a nature, which is accomplished by the soul's union with this terrestrial body. But in order to understand perfectly the secret meaning of the other parts of this fable, it will be necessary to give a more explicit detail of the particulars attending the abduction, from the beautiful poem of Claudian on this subject. From this elegant production we learn that Ceres, who was afraid lest some violence should be offered to Proserpina, on account of her inimitable beauty, conveyed her privately to Sicily, and concealed her in a house built on purpose by the Cyclopes, while she herself directs her course to the temple of Cybelé, the mother of the gods. Here, then, we see the first cause of the soul's descent, namely, the abandoning of a life wholly according to the higher intellect, which is occultly signified by, the separation of Proserpina from Ceres. Afterward, we are told that Jupiter instructs Venus to go to this abode, and betray Proserpina from her retirement, that Pluto may be enabled to carry her away; and to prevent any suspicion in the virgin's mind, he commands Diana and Pallas to go in company. The three goddesses arriving, find Proserpina at work on a scarf for her mother; in which she had embroidered the primitive chaos, and the formation of the world. Now by Venus in this part of the narration we must understand *desire*, which even in the celestial regions (for such is the residence of Proserpina till she is ravished by Pluto), begins silently and stealthily to creep into the recesses of the soul. By Minerva we must conceive *the rational power of the soul*, and by Diana, *nature*, or the merely natural and vegetable part of our composition; both which are now ensnared through the allurements of desire. And lastly, the web in which Proserpina had displayed all the fair variety of the material world, beautifully represents the commencement of the illusive operations through which the soul becomes ensnared with the beauty of imaginative forms. But let us for a while attend to the poet's elegant description of her employment and abode:

Venus, Diana, and Pallas visit Proserpina.

Devenere locum, Cereris quo tecta nitebant
Cyclopum firmata manu. Stant ardua ferro
Mænia; ferrati postes: immensaque nectit
Claustra chalybs. Nullum tanto sudore Pyracmon,
Nec Steropes, construxit opus: non talibus umquam
Spiravere Notis animæ nec flumine tanto
Incoctum maduit lassa cervice metallum.
Atria cingit ebur: trabibus solidatur aenis
Culmen et in celsas surgunt electra columnas.
Ipsa domum tenero mulcens Proserpina cantu
Irrita texebat redituræ munera matri.
Hic elementorum seriem sedesque paternas
Insignibat acu: veterem qua lege tumultum
Discrevit Natura parens et semina justis
Discessere locis: quidquid leve, fertur in altum,
In medium graviora cadunt, incanduit æther:
Egit flamma polum: fluxit mare: terra pependit
Nec color unus inest. Stellas accendit in auro,
Ostro fundit aquos, attollit litora gemmis,
Filaque mentitos jam jam cælantia fluctus
Arte tument. Credas inlidi cautibus algam,
Et raucum bibulis inserpere murmur arenis.
Addit quinque plagas: mediam subtemine rubro
Obsessam fervore notat: squalebat adustus
Limes et assiduo sitiebant stamina sole.
Vitales utrimque duas; quas mitis oberrat
Temperies habitanda viris. Tum fine supremo

Torpentes traxit geminas, brumaque perenni
Fædat, et æterno contristat frigore telas.
Nec non et patrui pingit sacraria Ditis,
Fatalesque sibi manes. Nec defuit omen.
Præscia nam subitis maduerunt fletibus ora.

After this, Proserpina, forgetful of her parent's commands, is represented as venturing from her retreat, through the treacherous persuasions of Venus:

Impulit Jonios præmisso lumine fluctus
Nondum pura dies: tremulis vibravit in undis
Ardor, et errantes ludunt per cærula flammæ.
Jamque audax animi, fidæque oblita parentis,
Fraude Dionæa riguos Proserpina saltus
(Sic Parcæ voluere) petit.

And this with the greatest propriety: for oblivion necessarily follows a remission of intellectual action, and is as necessarily attended with the allurements of desire. [145 80] Nor is her dress less symbolical of the acting of the soul in such a state, principally according to the energies and promptings of imagination and nature. For thus her garments are beautifully described by the poet:

Quas inter Cereris proles, nunc gloria matris,
Mox dolor, æquali tendit per gramina passu,
Nec membris nec honore minor; potuitque
Pallas, si clipeum, si ferret spicula, Phœbe.

Collectæ tereti nodantur jaspide vestes.
Pectinis ingenio nunquam felicior arti
Contigit eventus. Nullæ sic consona telæ
Fila, nec in tantum veri duxere figuram.
Hic Hyperionis Solem de semine nasci
Fecerat, et pariter, sed forma dispare lunam,
Auroræ noctisque duces. Cunabula Tethys
Præbet, et infantes gremio solatur anhelos,
Cæruleusque sinus roseis radiatur alumnis.
Invalidum dextro portat Titana lacerto
Nondum luce gravem, nec pubescentibus alte
Cristatum radiis: primo clementior ævo
Fingitur, et tenerum vagitu despuit ignem.
Læva parte soror vitrei libamina potat
Uberis, et parvo signatur tempora cornu.

In which description the sun represents the phantasy, and the moon, nature, as is well known to every tyro in the Platonic philosophy. They are likewise, with great propriety, described in their infantine state: for these energies do not arrive to perfection previous to the sinking of the soul into the dark receptacle of matter. After this we behold her issuing on the plain with Minerva and Diana, and attended by a beauteous train of nymphs, who are evident symbols of world of generation, [81] and are, therefore, the proper companions of the soul about to fall into its fluctuating realms.

But the design of Proserpina, in venturing from her retreat, is beautifully significant of her approaching descent: for she rambles from home for the purpose of gathering flowers; and this in a lawn replete with the most enchanting variety, and exhaling the most delicious odors. This is a manifest image of the soul operating principally according to the natural and external life, and so becoming effeminated and ensnared through the delusive attractions of sensible form. Minerva (the rational faculty in this case), likewise gives herself wholly to the dangerous employment, and abandons the proper characteristics of her nature for the destructive revels of desire.

All which is thus described with the utmost elegance by the poet:

Forma loci superat flores: curvata tumore
Parvo planities, et mollibus edita clivis
Creverat in collem. Vivo de pumice fontes
Roscida mobilibus lambebant gramina rivis.
Silvaque torrentes ramorum frigore soles
Temperat, et medio brumam sibi vindicat æstu.
Apta fretis abies, bellis accommoda cornus,
Quercus amica Jovi, tumulos tectura cupressus,
Ilex plena favis, venturi præscia laurus.
Fluctuat hic denso crispata cacumine buxus,
Hic ederæ serpunt, hic pampinus induit ulmos.
Haud procul inde lacus (Pergum dixere Sicani)
Panditur, et nemorum frondoso margine cinctus

Vicinis pallescit aquis: admittit in altum
Cernentes oculos, et late pervius humor
Ducit inoffensus liquido sub gurgite visus,
Imaque perspicui prodit secreta profundi.
Huc elapsa cohors gaudet per florida rura.
Hortatur Cytherea, legant. Nunc ite, sorores,
Dum matutinis præsudat solibus aer:
Dum meus humectat flaventes Lucifer agros,
Rotanti prævectus equo. Sic fata, doloris
Carpit signa sui. Varios tum cætera saltus
Invasere cohors. Credas examina fundi
Hyblæum raptura thymum, cum cerea reges
Castra movent, fagique cava dimissus ab alvo
Mellifer electis exercitus obstrepit herbis.
Pratorum spoliatur honos. Hac lilia fuscis
Intexit violis: hanc mollis amaracus ornat:
Hæc graditur stellata rosis; haec alba ligustris.
Te quoque, flebilibus mærens, Hyacinthe, figuris,
Narcissumque metunt, nunc inclita germina veris,
Prœstantes olim pueros. Tu natus Amyclis:
Hunc Helicon genuit. Te disci perculit error:
Hunc fontis decepit amor. Te fronte retusa
Delius, hunc fracta Cephissus arundine luget.
Æstuat ante alias avido fervore legendi
Frugiferæ spes una Deæ. Nunc vimine texto
Ridentes calathos spoliis agrestibus implet:
Nunc sociat flores seseque ignara coronat.

Augurium fatale tori. Quin ipsa tubarum
Armorumque potens, dextram, qua fortia turbat
Agmina, qua stabiles portas et mænia vellit,
Jam levibus laxat studiis hastamque reponit,
Insuetisque docet galeam mitescere sertis.
Ferratus lascivit apex horrorque recessit
Martius et cristæ pacato fulgure vernant.
Nec quæ Parthenium canibus scrutatur odorem,
Aspernata choros, libertatemque comarum
Injecta tantum voluit frenare corona.

Proserpina gathering Flowers.

But there is a circumstance relative to the narcissus which must not be passed over in silence: I mean its being, according to Ovid, the metamorphosis of a youth who fell a victim to the love of his own corporeal form; the secret meaning of which most admirably accords with the rape of Proserpina, which, according to Homer, was the immediate consequence of gathering this wonderful flower. [82] For by Narcissus falling in love with his shadow in the limpid stream we may behold an exquisitely apt representation of a soul vehemently gazing on the flowing condition of a material body, and in consequence of this, becoming enamored with a corporeal life, which is nothing more than the delusive image of the true man, or the rational and immortal soul. Hence, by an immoderate attachment to this unsubstantial mockery and gliding semblance of the real soul, such an one becomes, at length, wholly changed, as far as is possible to his nature, into a vegetive condition of being, into a beautiful but transient flower, that is, into a corporeal life, or a life totally consisting in the mere operations of nature. Proserpina, therefore, or the soul, at the very instant of her descent into matter, is, with the utmost propriety, represented as eagerly engaged in picking this fatal flower; for her faculties at this period are entirely occupied with a life divided about the fluctuating condition of body.

After this, Pluto, forcing his passage through the earth, seizes on Proserpina, and carries her away with him, notwithstanding the resistance of Minerva and Diana. They, indeed, are forbid by Jupiter, who in this place signifies Fate, to attempt her deliverance. By this resistance of Minerva and Diana no more is signified than that the lapse of the soul into a material nature is contrary to the genuine wish and proper condition, as well of the corporeal life depending on her essence, as of her true and rational nature. Well, therefore, may the soul, in such a situation, pathetically exclaim with Proserpina:

O male dilecti flores, despectaque matris
Consilia: O Veneris deprensæ serius artes![*]

Pluto carrying off Proserpina.

But, according to Minutius Felix, Proserpina was carried by Pluto through thick woods, and over a length of sea, and brought

---

* Oh flowers fatally dear, and the mother's cautions despised: Oh cruel arts of cunning Venus!

into a cavern, the residence of the dead: where by *woods* a material nature is plainly implied, as we have already observed in the first part of this discourse; and where the reader may likewise observe the agreement of the description in this particular with that of Virgil in the descent of his hero:

Tenent media omnia *silvæ*

Cocytusque sinuque labens, circumvenit atro.[*]

Proserpina brought before Pluto in Hades.

In these words the woods are expressly mentioned; and the ocean has an evident agreement with Cocytus, signifying the outflowing condition of a material nature, and the sorrows and sufferings attending its connection with the soul.

---

* "Woods cover all the middle space and Cocytus gliding on, surrounds it with his dusky bosom."

Pluto hurries Proserpina into the infernal regions: in other words, the soul is sunk into the profound depth and darkness of a material nature. A description of her marriage next succeeds, her union with the dark tenement of the body:

Jam suus inferno processerat Hesperus orbi
Ducitur in thalamum virgo. Stat pronuba juxta
Stellantes Nox pieta sinus, tangensque cubile
Omina perpetuo genitalia federe sancit.

Night is with great beauty and propriety introduced as standing by the nuptial couch, and confirming the oblivious league. For the soul through her union with a material body becomes an inhabitant of darkness, and subject to the empire of night; in consequence of which she dwells wholly with delusive phantoms, and till she breaks her fetters is deprived of the intuitive perception of that which is real and true.

In the next place, we are presented with the following beautiful and pathetic description of Proserpina appearing in a dream to Ceres, and bewailing her captive and miserable condition:

Sed tunc ipsa sui jam non ambagibus ullis
Nuntia, materna facies ingesta sopori.
Namque videbatur tenebroso obtecta recessu
Carceris, et sævis Proserpina vincta catenis,
Non qualem roseis nuper convallibus Ætnæ
Suspexere Deæ. Squalebat pulchrior auro

Cæsaries, et nox oculorum infecerat ignes.

Exhaustusque gelu pallet rubor. Ille superbi

Flammeus oris honos, et non cessura pruinis

Membra colorantur picei caligine regni.

Ergo hanc ut dubio vix tandem agnoscere visu

Evaluit: cujus tot pænæ criminis? inquit.

Unde hæc informis macies? Cui tanta facultas

In me sævitiæ est? Rigidi cur vincula ferri

Vix aptanda feris molles meruere lacerti?

Tu, mea tu proles?

An vana fallimur umbra?

Such, indeed, is the wretched situation of the soul when profoundly merged in a corporeal nature. She not only becomes captive and fettered, but loses all her original splendor; she is defiled with the impurity of matter; and the sharpness of her rational sight is blunted and dimmed through the thick darkness of a material night. The reader may observe how Proserpina, being represented as confined in the dark recess of a prison, and bound with fetters, confirms the explanation of the fable here given as symbolical of the descent of the soul; for such, as we have already largely proved, is the condition of the soul from its union with the body, according to the uniform testimony of the most ancient philosophers and priests. [83]

After this, the wanderings of Ceres for the discovery of Proserpina commence. She is described, by Minutius Felix, as begirt with a serpent, and bearing two lighted torches in her hands; but by Claudian, instead of being girt with a serpent, she commences her search by night in a car drawn by dragons. But the meaning of the allegory is the same in each; for both a serpent and a dragon are emblems of a divisible life subject to transitions and changes, with which, in this case, our intellectual (and diviner) part becomes connected: since as these animals put off their skins, and become young again, so the divisible life of the soul, falling into generation, is rejuvenized in its subsequent career. But what emblem can more beautifully represent the evolutions and outgoings of an intellectual nature into the regions of sense than the wanderings of Ceres by the light of torches through the darkness of night, and continuing the pursuit until she proceeds into the depths of Hades itself? For the intellectual part of the soul, [84] when it verges towards body, enkindles, indeed, a light in its dark receptacle, but becomes itself situated in obscurity: and, as Proclus somewhere divinely observes, the mortal nature by this means participates of the divine intellect, but the intellectual part is drawn down to death. The tears and lamentations too, of Ceres, in her course, are symbolical both of the providential operations of intellect about a mortal nature, and the miseries with which such operations are (with respect to imperfect souls like ours) attended. Nor is it without reason that Iacchus, or Bacchus, is celebrated by Orpheus as the companion of her search: for Bacchus is the evident symbol of the imperfect energies of intellect, and its scattering into the obscure and lamentable dominions of sense.

But our explanation will receive additional strength from considering that these sacred rites occupied the space of nine days in their celebration; and this, doubtless, because, according to Homer, [85] this goddess did not discover the residence of her daughter till the expiration of that period. For the soul, in falling from her original and divine abode in the heavens, passed through eight spheres, namely, the fixed or inerratic sphere, and the seven planets,

Ceres before Pluto.

assuming a different body, and employing different faculties in each; and becomes connected with the sublunary world and a terrene body, as the ninth, and most abject gradation of her descent. Hence the first day of initiation into these mystic rites was called *agurmos, i. e.* according to Hesychius, *ekklesia* et παν το αγειρομενον, *an assembly, and all collecting together:* and this with the greatest propriety; for, according to Pythagoras, "the people of dreams are souls collected together in the Galaxy. [86] Δημος δε ονειρων κατα Πυθαγοραν αί ψυχαι, άς συναγεσθαι φησιν εις τον γαλαξιαν. [87] And from this part of the heavens souls first begin to descend. After this, the soul falls from the tropic of Cancer into the planet Saturn; and to this the second day of initiation was consecrated, which they called Αλαδε μυσται, ["to the sea, ye initiated ones!"] because, says Meursius, on that day the crier was accustomed to admonish the mystæ to betake themselves to the sea. Now the meaning of this will be easily understood, by considering that, according to the arcana of the ancient theology, as may be learned from Proclus, [88] the whole planetary system is under the dominion of Neptune; and this too is confirmed by Martianus Capella, who describes the several planets as so many streams. Hence when the soul falls into the planet Saturn, which Capella compares to a river voluminous, sluggish, and cold, she then first merges herself into fluctuating matter, though purer than that of a sublunary nature, and of which water is an ancient and significant symbol. Besides, the sea is an emblem of purity, as is evident from the Orphic hymn to Ocean, in which that deity is called θεων αγνισμα μεγιστον, *theon agnisma megiston*, i. e. *the greatest purifier of the gods:* and Saturn, as we have already observed, is *pure* [intuitive] *intellect.* And what still more confirms this observation is, that Pythagoras, as we are informed by Porphyry, in his life of that philosopher, symbolically called the sea *a tear of Saturn.* But the eighth day of initiation, which is symbolical of the falling of the soul into the lunar orb, [89] was celebrated by the candidates by a *repeated initiation and second sacred rites;* because the soul in this situation is about to bid adieu to every thing of a celestial nature; to sink into a perfect oblivion of her divine origin and pristine felicity; and to rush profoundly into the region of dissimilitude, [90] ignorance, and error.

And lastly, on the ninth day, when the soul falls into the sublunary world and becomes united with a terrestrial body, a libation was performed, such as is usual in sacred rites. Here the initiates, filling two earthen vessels of broad and spacious bottoms, which were called πλημοχοαι, *plemokhoai*, and κοτυλυσκοι, *kotuluskoi*, the former of these words denoting vessels of a conical shape, and the latter small bowls or cups sacred to Bacchus, they placed one towards the east, and the other towards the west. And the first of these was doubtless, according to the interpretation of Proclus, sacred to the earth, and symbolical of the soul proceeding from an orbicular figure, or divine form, into a conical defluxion and terrene situation: [91] but the other was sacred to the soul, and symbolical of its celestial origin: since our intellect is the legitimate progeny of Bacchus. And this too was occultly signified by the position of the earthen vessels; for, according to a mundane distribution of the divinities, the eastern center of the universe, which is analogous to fire, belongs to Jupiter, who likewise governs the fixed and inerratic sphere; and the western to Pluto, who governs the earth, because the west is allied to earth on account of its dark and nocturnal nature. [92]

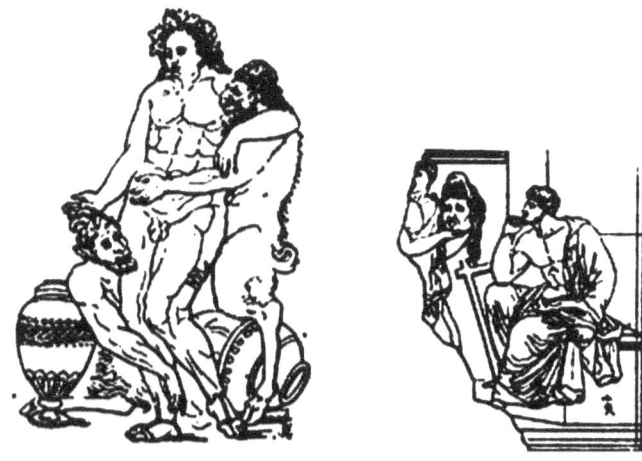

Bacchus and Faun. Tragic Actor.

Group of Greek Divinities.

Goddess Night. Three Graces.

Again, according to Clemens Alexandrinus, the following confession was made by the new initiate in these sacred rites, in answer to the interrogations of the Hierophant: "I have fasted; I have drank the Cyceon; [93] I have taken out of the Cista, and placed what I have taken out into the Calathus; and alternately I have taken out of the Calathus and put into the Cista." Καστι το συνθημα Ελευσινιων μυστηριων. Ενηστωσα· επιον τον κυκεωνα· ελαβον εκ κιστης, εργασαμενοςαπεθεμην εις καλαθον, και εκ καλαθου εις κιστην. But as this pertains to a circumstance attending the wanderings of Ceres, which formed the most mystic and emblematical part of the ceremonies, it is necessary to adduce the following arcane narration, summarily collected from the writings of Arnobius: "The goddess Ceres, when searching through the earth for her daughter, in the course of her wanderings arrived at the boundaries of Eleusis, in the Attic region, a place which was then inhabited by a people called *Autochthones*, or descended from the earth, whose names were as follows: Baubo and Triptolemus; Dysaules, a goatherd; Eubulus, a keeper of swine; and Eumolpus, a shepherd, from whom the race of the Eumolpidæ descended, and the illustrious name of Cecropidæ was derived; and who afterward flourished as bearers of the caduceus, hierophants, and criers belonging to the sacred rites. Baubo, therefore, who was of the female sex, received Ceres, wearied with complicated evils, as her guest, and endeavored to soothe her sorrows by obsequious and flattering attendance. For this purpose she entreated her to pay attention to the refreshment of her body, and placed before her *a mixed potion* to assuage the vehemence of her thirst. But the sorrowful goddess was averse from her solicitations, and rejected the friendly officiousness of the hospitable dame. The matron, however, who was not easily repulsed, still continued her entreaties, which were as obstinately resisted by Ceres, who persevered in her refusal with unshaken persistency and invincible firmness. But when Baubo had thus often exerted her endeavours to appease the sorrows of Ceres, but without any effect, she, at length, changed her arts, and determined to try if she could not exhilarate, by prodigies (or out-of-the-way expedients), a mind which she was not able to allure by earnest endeavors. For this purpose she uncovered that part of her body by which the female sex produces children and derives the appellation of woman. [94] This she caused to assume a purer appearance, and a smoothness such as is found in the private parts of a stripling child. She then returns to the afflicted goddess, and, in the midst of those attempts which are usually employed to alleviate distress, she uncovers herself, and exhibits her secret parts; upon which the goddess fixed her eyes, and was diverted with the novel method of mitigating the anguish of sorrow; and afterward, becoming more cheerful through laughter, she assuages her thirst with the mingled potion which she had before despised." Thus far Arnobius; and the same narration is epitomized by Clemens Alexandrinus, who is very indignant at the indecency as he conceives, in the story, and because it composed the arcana of the Eleusinian rites. Indeed as the simple father, with the usual ignorance [95] of a Christian priest, considered the fable literally, and as designed to promote indecency and lust, we can not wonder at his ill-timed abuse.

But the fact is, this narration belonged to the ἀπόρρητα, *aporrheta*, or arcane discourses, on account of its mystical meaning, and to prevent it from becoming the object of ignorant declamation, licentious perversion, and impious contempt. For the purity and excellence of these institutions is perpetually acknowledged even by Dr. Warburton himself, who, in this instance, has dispersed, for a moment, the mists of delusion and intolerant zeal. [96] Besides, as Iamblichus beautifully observes, [97] "exhibitions of this kind in the Mysteries were designed to free us from licentious passions, by gratifying the sight, and at the same time vanquishing desire, through the awful sanctity with which these rites were accompanied: for," says he, "the proper way of freeing ourselves from the passions is, first, to indulge them with moderation, by which means they become satisfied; listen, as it were, to persuasion, and may thus be entirely removed." [98] This doctrine is indeed so rational, that it can never be objected to by any but quacks in philosophy and religion. For as he is nothing more than a quack in medicine who endeavors to remove a latent bodily disease before he has called it forth externally, and by this means diminished its fury; so he is nothing more than a pretender in philosophy who attempts to remove the passions by violent repression, instead of moderate compliance and gentle persuasion.

But to return from this disgression, the following appears to be the secret meaning of this mystic discourse: The matron Baubo may be considered as a symbol of that passive, womanish, and corporeal life through which the soul becomes united with this earthly body, and through which, being at first ensnared, it descended, and, as it

Cupid and Venus. Satyr and Goat. Baubo, Ceres, and Nymphs.

were, was born into the world of generation, passing, by this means, from mature perfection, splendor and reality, into infancy, darkness, and error. Ceres, therefore, or the intellectual soul, in the course of her wanderings, that is, of her evolutions and goings-forth into matter, is at length captivated with the arts of Baubo, or a corporeal life, and forgets her sorrows, that is, imbibes oblivion of her wretched state in the mingled potion which she prepares: the mingled liquor being an obvious symbol of such a life, mixed and impure, and, on this account, liable to corruption and death; since every thing pure and unmixed is incorruptible and divine. And here it is necessary to caution the reader from imagining, that because, according to the fable, the wanderings of Ceres commence after the rape of Proserpina, hence the intuitive intellect descends subsequently to the soul, and separate from it. Nothing more is meant by this circumstance than that the diviner intellect, from the superior excellence of its nature, has in cause, though not in time, a priority to soul, and that on this account a defection and revolt (and descent earthward from the heavenly condition) commences, from the soul, and afterward takes place in the intellect, yet so that the former descends with the latter in inseparable attendance.

From this explanation, then, of the fable, we may easily perceive the meaning of the mystic confession, *I have fasted; I have drank a mingled potion,* etc.; for by the former part of the assertion, no more is meant than that the higher intellect, previous to imbibing of oblivion through the deceptive arts of a corporeal life, abstains from all material concerns, and does not mingle itself (as far as its nature is capable of such abasement) with even the necessary delights of the body. And as to the latter part, it doubtless alludes to the descent of Proserpina to Hades, and her re-ascent to the abodes of her mother Ceres: that is, to the outgoing and return of the soul, alternately falling into generation, and ascending thence into the intelligible world, and becoming perfectly restored to her divine and intellectual nature. For *the Cista* contained the most arcane symbols of the Mysteries, into which it was unlawful for the profane to look: and whatever were its contents, [99] we learn from the hymn of Callimachus to Ceres, that they were formed from gold, which, from its incorruptibility, is an evident symbol of an immaterial nature. And as to the Calathus, or basket, this, as we are told by Claudian, was filled with *spoliis agrestibus, the spoils or fruits of the field*, which are manifest symbols of a life corporeal and earthly. So that the candidate, by confessing that he had taken from the Cista, and placed what he had taken into the Calathus, and the contrary, occultly acknowledged the descent of his soul from a condition of being super-material and immortal, into one material and mortal; and that, on the contrary, by living according to the purity which the Mysteries inculcated, he should re-ascend to that perfection of his nature, from which he had unhappily fallen. [100]

It only now remains that we consider the last part of this fabulous narration, or arcane discourse. It is said, that after the goddess Ceres, on arriving at Eleusis, had discovered her daughter, she instructed the Eleusinians in the planting of corn: or, according to Claudian, the search of Ceres for her daughter, through the goddess, instructing in the art of tillage as she went, proved the occasion of a universal benefit to mankind. Now the secret meaning of this will be obvious, by considering that the descent of the superior intellect into the realms of generated existence becomes, indeed, the greatest benefit and ornament which a material nature is capable of receiving: for without this participation of intellect in the lowest department of corporeal life, nothing but the irrational soul [101] and a brutal life would subsist in its dark and fluctuating abode, the body. As the art of tillage, therefore, and particularly the growing of corn, becomes the greatest possible benefit to our sensible life, no symbol can more aptly represent the unparalleled advantages arising from the evolution and procession of intellect with its divine nature into a corporeal life, than the good resulting from agriculture and corn: for whatever of horrid and dismal can be conceived in night, supposing it to be perpetually destitute of the friendly illuminations of the moon and stars, such, and infinitely more dreadful, would be the condition of an earthly nature, if deprived of the beneficent irradiations [προοδοι] and supervening benefits of the diviner life.

And this much for an explanation of the Eleusinian Mysteries, or the history of Ceres and Proserpina; in which it must be remembered that as this fable, according to the excellent observation of Sallust already adduced, is of the mixed kind, though the descent of the soul was doubtless principally alluded to by these sacred rites, yet they likewise occultly signified, agreeable to the nature of the fable, the descending of divinity into the sublunary world. But when we view the fable in this part of its meaning, *we must be careful not to confound the nature of a partial intellect like ours with the one universal and divine.* As everything subsisting about the gods is divine, therefore intellect in the highest degree, and next to this soul, and hence wanderings and abductions, lamentations and tears, can here only signify the participations and providential operations of these in inferior natures; and this in such a manner as not to derogate from the dignity, or impair the perfection, of the divine principle thus imparted. I only add, that the preceding exposition will enable us to perceive the meaning and beauty of the following representation of the rape of Proserpina, from the Heliacan tables of Hieronymus Aleander. [102] Here, first of all, we behold Ceres in a car drawn by two dragons, and afterwards, Diana and Minerva, with an inverted calathus at their feet, and pointing out to Ceres her daughter Proserpina, who is hurried away by Pluto in his car, and is in the attitude of one struggling to be free. Hercules is likewise represented with his club, in the attitude of opposing the violence of Pluto: and last of all, Jupiter is represented extending his hand, as if willing to assist Proserpina in escaping from the embraces of Pluto. I shall therefore conclude this section with the following remarkable passage from Plutarch, which will not only confirm, but be itself corroborated by the preceding exposition. Ότι μεν ουν ή παλαια φυσιολογια, και παρ Ελλησι και Βαρβαροις, λογος ήν φυσικος ελκεκαλυμμενος μυθοις, τα πολλα δι' αινιγματων και ύπονοιων επικρυφος, και μυστηριωδης θεολογια. Τα τε λαλουμενα των σιγωμενων σαφεστερα τοις πολλοις εχοντα. Και τα σιγωμενα των λαλουμενων ύποπτοτερα. Δηλον εστι, pergit, εν τοις Ορφικοις επεσι, και τοις Αιγυπτιακοις και Φρυγιοις λογοις. Μαλιστα δε οί περι τας τελετας οργιασμοι, και τα δρωμενα συμβολικως εν ταις ίερουργιαις, την των παλαιων εμφαιναι διανοιαν. [103] *i. e.* "The ancient physiology, [104] both of the Greeks and the *Barbarians*, was nothing else than a discourse on natural subjects, involved or veiled in fables, concealing many things through enigmas and under-meanings, and also a theology taught, in which, after the manner of the Mysteries, [105] the things spoken were clearer to the multitude than those delivered in silence, and the things delivered in silence were more subject to investigation than what was spoken. This is manifest from the *Orphic verses*, and the Egyptian and Phrygian discourses. *But the orgies of initiations, and the symbolical ceremonies of sacred rites especially, exhibit the understanding had of them by the ancients.*"

FOOTNOTES

10. The profounder esoteric doctrines of the ancients were denominated *wisdom*, and afterward *philosophy*, and also the *gnosis* or knowledge. They related to the human soul, its divine parentage, its supposed degradation from its high estate by becoming connected with "generation" or the physical world, its onward progress and restoration to God by regenerations, popularly supposed to be transmigrations, etc.—A. W.

11. *Stromata*, book iii.

12. *Commentary on the Statesman of Plato*, page 374.

13. The Lesser Mysteries were celebrated at Agræ; and the persons there initiated were denominated *Mystæ*: Only such could be received at the sacred rites at Eleusis.

14. Philosophy here relates to discipline of the life.

15. Greek μαντεις *manteis*—more properly prophets, those filled by the prophetic mania or eutheasm.

16. More correctly—"The soul is yoked to the body as if by way of punishment," as culprits were fastened to others or even to corpses. See *Paul's Epistle to the Romans*, vii, 25.

17. Greek ὑλη, matter supposed to contain all the principles the negative of life, order, and goodness.

18. This passage doubtless alludes to the ancient and beautiful story of Cupid and Psyché, in which Psyché is said to fall asleep in Hades; and this through rashly attempting to behold corporeal beauty: and the observation of Plotinus will enable the profound and contemplative reader to unfold the greater part of the mysteries contained in this elegant fable. But, prior to Plotinus, Plato, in the seventh book of his *Republic*, asserts that such as are unable in the present life to apprehend *the idea of the good*, will descend to Hades after death, and fall asleep in its dark abodes. Ός αν μη εχη διορισασθαι τῳ λογῳ, απο των αλλων παντων αφελων την του αγαθου ιδεαν, και ωσπερ εν μαχη δια παντων ελεγχων διεξιων, με κατα δοξαν αλλα κατ' ουσιαν προθυμουμενος ελεγχειν, εν πασι τουτοις απτωτι τῳ λογῳ διαπορευηται, ουτε αυτο το αγαθον ουδεν φησεις ειδεναι τον ουτως εχοντα, ουτε αλλο αγαθον ουδεν; αλλ' ει πη ειδωλου τινος εφαπτεται, δοξη ουκ επιστημη εφαπτεσθαι; και τον νυν βιον ονειροπολουντα, και ὑπνωτοντα, πριν ενθαδ' εξεργεσθαι; εις ᾳδου προτερον αφικομενον τελεως επικαταδαρθανειν; *i. e.* "He who is not able, by the exercise of his reason, *to define the idea of the good*, separating it from all other objects, and piercing, as in a battle, through every kind of argument; endeavoring to confute, not according to opinion, but according to essence, and proceeding through all these dialectical energies with an unshaken reason;—he who can not accomplish this, would you not say, that he neither knows the good itself, nor anything which is properly denominated good? And would you not assert that such a one, when he apprehends any certain image of reality, apprehends it rather through the medium of opinion than of science; that in the present life he is sunk in sleep, and conversant with the delusion of dreams; and that before he is roused to a vigilant state he will descend to Hades, and be overwhelmed with a sleep perfectly profound."
Henry Davis translates this passage more critically: "Is not the ease the same with reference to the good? Whoever can not logically define it, abstracting the idea of *the good* from all others, and taking, as in a fight, one opposing argument after another, and can not proceed with unfailing proofs, eager to rest his ease, not on the ground of opinion, but of true being,—such a one knows nothing of *the good itself*, nor of any good whatever; and should he have attained to any knowledge of *the good*, we must

say that he has attained it by opinion, not by science (επιστημη); that he is sleeping and dreaming away his present life; and before he is roused will descend to Hades, and there be profoundly and perfectly laid asleep." vii. 14.

19. *Phædo*, 38. "Those who instituted the Mysteries for us appear to have intimated that whoever shall arrive in Hades unpurified and not initiated shall lie in mud; but he who arrives there purified and initiated shall dwell with the gods. For there are many bearers of the wand or thyrsus, but few who are inspired."

20. *Intellect*, Greek νους, *nous*, is the higher faculty of the mind. It is substantially the same as the *pneuma*, or spirit, treated of in the New Testament; and hence the term "*intellectual*," as used in Mr. Taylor's translation of the Platonic writers, may be pretty safely read as spiritual, by those familiar with the Christian cultus.—A. W.

21. *Physics of Aristotle*.

22. Ficinus: *De Immortal. Anim.* book xviii.

23. We observe in the *New Testament* a like disposition on the part of Jesus and Paul to classify their doctrines as esoteric and exoteric, "the Mysteries of the kingdom of God" for the apostles, and "parables" for the multitude. "We speak wisdom," says Paul, "among them that are perfect" (or initiated), etc. 1 *Corinthians*, ii. Also Jesus declares: "It is given to you to know the Mysteries of the kingdom of heaven, but to them it is not given; therefore I speak to them in parables: because they seeing, see not, and hearing, they hear not, neither do they understand."—*Matthew* xiii., 11-13. He also justified the withholding of the higher and interior knowledge from the untaught and ill-disposed, in the memorable *Sermon on the Mount.*—*Matthew* vii.:
"Give ye not that which is sacred to the dogs,
Neither cast ye your pearls to the swine;
For the swine will tread them under their feet
And the dogs will turn and rend you."
This same division of the Christians into neophytes and perfect, appears to have been kept up for centuries; and Godfrey Higgins asserts that it is maintained in the Roman Church.—A. W.

24. Herodotus, ii. 51, 81.
"What Orpheus delivered in hidden allegories Pythagoras learned when he was initiated into the Orphic Mysteries; and Plato next received a knowledge of them from the Orphic and Pythagorean writings."

25. *Ancient Symbol-Worship*, page 11, *note*.

26. *I. e.*, a disposition to investigate for the purpose of eliciting truth, and reducing it to practice.

27. Cocytus, lamentation, a river in the Underworld.

28. Jacob Bryant says: "All fountains were esteemed sacred, but especially those which had any preternatural quality and abounded with exhalations. It was an universal notion that a divine energy proceeded from these effluvia; and that the persons who resided in their vicinity were gifted with a prophetic quality. . . . The Ammonians styled such fountains *Ain Omphé*, or fountains of the oracle; ομφη, *omphé*, signifying 'the voice of God.' These terms the Greeks contracted to Νυμφη, *numphe*, a nymph."—*Ancient Mythology*, vol. i. p. 276.
The Delphic oracle was above a fissure, *gounous* or *bocca inferiore*, of the earth, and the pythoness inhaled the vapors.—A. W.

29. *Republic*. x, 16. "After they were laid asleep, and midnight was approaching, there was

thunder and earthquake; and they were thence on a sudden carried upward, some one way, and some another, approaching to the region of generation like stars."

30. *Material* demons are a lower grade of spiritual essences that are capable of assuming forms which make them perceptible by the physical senses.—A. W.

31. *Hyle* or Matter. All evil incident to human life, as is here shown, was supposed to originate from the connection of the soul to material substance, the latter being regarded as the receptacle of everything evil. But why the soul is thus immerged and punished is nowhere explained.—A. W.

32. This and the other citations from Empedocles are to be found in the book of Hierocles on *The Golden Verses* of Pythagoras.

33. The presence of Cerberus in Grecian and Roman descriptions of the Underworld shows that the ideas of the poets and mythologists were derived, not only from Egypt, but from the Brahmans of the far East. Yama, the lord of the Underworld, is attended by his dog *Karbaru*, the spotted, styled also *Trikasa*, the three-headed.

34. In the second edition these terms are changed to *dianoietic* and *doxastic*, words which we cannot adopt, as they are not accepted English terms. The *nous*, intellect or spirit, pertains to the higher or intuitional part of the mind; the *dianoia* or understanding to the reasoning faculty, and the *doxa*, or opinion-forming power, to the faculty of investigation.—Plotinus, accepting this theory of mind, says: "Knowledge has three degrees—opinion, science, and illumination. The means or instrument of the first is reception; of the second, dialectic; of the third, intuition."—A. W.

35. Hades, the Underworld, supposed by classical students to be the region or estate of departed souls, it will have been noticed, is regarded by Mr. Taylor and other Platonists, as the human body, which they consider to be the grave and place of punishment of the soul.—A. W.

36. *Aporrheta*, the arcane or confidential disclosures made to the candidate undergoing initiation. In the Eleusinia, these were made by the Hierophant, and enforced by him from the Book of Interpretation, said to have consisted of two tablets of stone. This was the *petroma*, a name usually derived from *petra*, a rock, or possibly from, *peter*, an interpreter. See *II. Corinthians*, xii. 6-8.—A. W.

37. *Phædo*, 16. "The instruction in the doctrine given in the Mysteries, that we human beings are in a kind of prison, and that we ought not to free ourselves from it or seek to escape, appears to me difficult to be understood, and not easy to apprehend. The gods take care of us, and we are theirs."
   Plotinus, it will be remembered, perceived by the interior faculty that Porphyry contemplated suicide, and admonished him accordingly.—A. W.

38. In the Hindu mythology, from which this symbolism is evidently derived, a deity deprived thus of the lingam or phallus, parted with his divine authority.

39. From Dionysus, the Greek name of Bacchus, and usually so translated.

40. *Commentary on the Statesman of Plato, p.* 382.

41. *Theology of Plato*, book iv. p. 220.

42. Theon appears to regard the final apocalypse or epopteia, like E. Pococke to whose views allusion is made elsewhere. This writer says: "The initiated were styled ebaptoi," and adds in a foot-note—"*Avaptoi*, literally obtaining or getting." According to this the *epopteia* would imply the final reception of the interior doctrines.—A. W.

43. The apostle Paul apparently alludes to the disclosing of the Mystical doctrines to the epopts or seers, in his *Second Epistle to the Corinthians*, xii. 3, 4: "I knew a certain man,—

whether in body or outside of body, I know not: God knoweth,—who was rapt into paradise, and heard αρρητα ρηματα, things ineffable, which it is not lawful for a man to repeat."

44. PAUL, *Epistle to the Philippians*, iii, 20: "Our citizenship is in the heavens."

45. *Medical and Surgical Reporter*, vol. xxxii. p. 195. "Those who have professed to teach their fellow-mortals new truths concerning immortality, have based their authority on direct divine inspiration. Numa, Zoroaster, Mohammed, Swedenborg, all claimed communication with higher spirits; they were what the Greeks called *entheast*—'immersed in God'—a striking word which Byron introduced into our tongue." Carpenter describes the condition as an automatic action of the brain. The inspired ideas arise in the mind suddenly, spontaneously, but very vividly, at some time when *thinking of some other topic*. Francis Galton defines genius as "the automatic activity of the mind, as distinguished from the effort of the will,—the ideas coming by inspiration." This action, says the editor of the *Reporter*, is largely favored by a condition approaching mental disorder—at least by one remote from the ordinary working day habits of thought. Fasting, prolonged intense mental action, great and unusual commotion of mind, will produce it; and, indeed, these extraordinary displays seem to have been so preceded. Jesus, Buddha, Mohammed, all began their careers by fasting, and visions of devils followed by angels. The candidates in the Eleusinian Mysteries also saw visions and apparitions, while engaged in the mystic orgies. We do not, however, accept the materialistic view of this subject. The cases are *entheastic;* and although hysteria and other disorders of the sympathetic system sometimes imitate the phenomena, we believe with Plato and Plotinus, that the higher faculty, intellect or intuition as we prefer to call it, the noetic part of our nature, is the faculty actually at work. "By reflection, self-knowledge, and intellectual discipline, the soul can be raised to the vision of eternal truth, goodness, and beauty—that is, to the vision of God." This is the epopteia.—A. W.

46. PLATO: *Republic*, vi. 5. "He who possesses the love of true knowledge is naturally carried in his aspirations to the real principle of being; and his love knows no repose till t shall have been united with the essence of each object through that part of the soul, which is akin to the Permanent and Essential; and so, the divine conjunction having evolved interior knowledge and truth, the knowledge of being is won."

47. *Timæus*. xliv. "The Deity (Demiurgus) himself formed the *divine*; and then delivered over to his celestial offspring [the subordinate or generated gods], the task of creating the *mortal*. These subordinate deities, copying the example of their parent, and receiving from his hands the *immortal principles* of the human soul, fashioned after this the mortal body, which they consigned to the soul as a vehicle, and in which they placed also another kind of a soul, which is mortal, and is the seat of violent and fatal passions."

48. That is to say, as if dying. Koré was a name of Proserpina.

49. *I. e.* as if divided into pieces.

50. *I. e.* Chained fast.

51. I *Corinthians*, xv. 42-44. "So also is the *anastasis* of the dead. It is sown in corruption [the material body]; it is raised in incorruption: it is sown in dishonor; it is raised in glory: it is sown in weakness; it is raised in power: it is sown a psychical body; it is raised a spiritual body."

52. *The Golden Ass*. xi. p. 239 (*Bohn*).

53. The peculiar rites of the Mysteries were indifferently termed Orgies or Labors, *teletai* or finishings, and initiations.

54. *Phædrus*, 64.

55. PROCLUS: *Theology of Plato*, book iv. The following reading is suggested: "The initiation and final disclosing are a symbol of the Ineffable Silence, and of the *enosis*, or being at one and *en rapport* with the mystical verities through manifestations intuitively comprehended."

    The μυησις, *muesis*, or initiation is defined by E. Pococke as relating to the "well-known Buddhist Moksha, final and eternal happiness, the liberation of the soul from the body and its exemption from further transmigration." For all *mystæ* therefore there was a certain welcome to the abodes of the blessed. The term εποπτεια, *epopteia*, applied to the last scene of initiation, he derives from the Sanscrit, *evaptoi*, an obtaining; the epopt being regarded as having secured for himself or herself divine bliss.

    It is more usual, however, to treat these terms as pure Greek; and to render the *muesis* as initiation and to derive *epopteia* from εποπτομαι. According to this etymology an epopt is a *seer* or *clairvoyant*, one who knows the interior wisdom. The terms inspector and superintendent do not, to me, at all express the idea, and I am inclined, in fact, to suppose with Mr. Pococke, that the Mysteries came from the East, and from that to deduce that the technical words and expressions are other than Greek.

    Plotinus, speaking of this *enosis* or oneness, lays down a spiritual discipline analogous to that of the Mystic Orgies: "Purify your soul from all undue hope and fear about earthly things; mortify the body, deny self,—affections as well as appetites,—and the inner eye will begin to exercise its clear and solemn vision." "In the reduction of your soul to its simplest principles, the divine germ, you attain this oneness. We stand then in the immediate presence of God, who shines out from the profound depths of the soul."—A. W.

56. APULEIUS: *The Golden Ass*. xi. The candidate was instructed by the hierophant, and permitted to look within the *cista* or chest, which contained the mystic serpent, the phallus, egg, and grains sacred to Demeter. As the epopt was reverent, or otherwise, he now "knew himself" by the sentiments aroused. Plato and Alcibiades gazed with emotions wide apart.—A. W.

57. PLOTINUS: *Letter to Flaccus*. "It is only now and then that we can enjoy the elevation made possible for us, above the limits of the body and the world. I myself have realized it but three times as yet, and Porphyry hitherto not once."

    Porphyry afterward declared that he witnessed four times, when near him, the soul or "intellect "of Plotinus thus raised up to the First and Sovereign Good; also that he himself was only once so elevated to the *enosis* or union with God, so as to have glimpses of the eternal world. This did not occur till he was sixty-eight years of age.—A. W.

58. *I. e.* a luminous appearance without any defined form or shape of an object.

59. *Commentary upon the Republic of Plato*, page 380.

60. *Ennead*, i. book 6; and ix. book 9.

61. Plotinus, Porphyry, Iamblichus, Proclus, Longinus, and their associates.

62. *Epilepsy*.

63. *Divine Legation*, p. 231.

64. *I. e.* The Mother-Goddess, Isis or Demeter, symbolized as Selene or the Moon.

65. *I. e.* to its former divine condition.

66. We have taken the liberty to present the following version of this passage, as more correctly expressing the sense of the original: "At the holy places are first the public purifications. With these the more arcane exercises follow; and after those the obligations (συστασεις) are taken, and the initiations follow, ending with the *epoptic* disclosures. So, as will be seen, the moral and social (political) virtues are analogous to the public purifications; the purifying virtues in their turn, which take the place of all external matters, correspond to the more arcane disciplines; the contemplative exercises concerning things to be known intuitively to the taking of the obligations; the including of them as an undivided whole, to the initiations; and the simple ocular view of simple objects to the epoptic revelations."

67. The writings of Augustin handed Neo-Platonism down to posterity as the original and esoteric doctrine of the first followers of Plato. He enumerates the causes which led, in his opinion, to the negative position assumed by the Academics, and to the concealment of their real opinions. He describes Plotinus as a resuscitated Plato.— *Against the Academics*, iii. 17-20.

68. *Phædo*, 21. Κινδυνευουσι γαρ ὁσοι τυγχανουσιν ορθως απτομενοι φιλοσοφιας λεληθεναι τας αλλους, ὁτι ουδεν αλλο αὑτοι επιτηδευουσιν ἡ αποθνησκειν τε και τεθναναι. *I. e.* For as many as rightly apply themselves to philosophy seem to have left others ignorant, that they themselves aim at nothing else than to die and to be dead. Elsewhere (31) Socrates says: "While we live, we shall approach nearest to intuitive knowledge, if we hold no communion with the body, except, what absolute necessity requires, nor suffer ourselves to be pervaded by its nature, but purify ourselves from it until God himself shall release us."

69. It is to be regretted, nevertheless, that our author had not risked the "danger and drudgery" of learning Greek, so as to have rendered fuller justice to his subject, and been of greater service to his readers. We are conscious that those who are too learned in verbal criticism are prone to overlook the real purport of the text.—A. W.

70. APULEIUS: *The Golden Ass. (Story of Cupid and Psyche)*, book vi.

71. Chests or baskets, made of osiers, in which were enclosed the mystical images and utensils which the uninitiated were not permitted to behold.

72. *I. e.* as to death; analogously to the descent of Koré-Persephoné to the Underworld.

73. *De Diis et Mundo*, p. 251.

74. *Evang. Præpar.* book iii. chap. 2.

75. Coric from Κορη, *Koré*, a name of Proserpina. The name is derived by E. Pococke from the Sanscrit *Gourè*.

76. PROCLUS: *Theology of Plato*, p. 371.

77. Plotinus taught the existence of three hypostases in the Divine Nature. There was the Demiurge, the God of Creation and Providence; the Second, the Intelligible, self-contained and immutable Source of life; and above all, the One, who like the *Zervané Akerené* of the Persians, is above all Being, a pure will, an Absolute Love— "Intellect."—A. W.

78. Also denominated by Kant, *Pure reason*, and by Prof. Cocker, *Intuitive reason*. It was considered by Plato, as "not amenable to the conditions of time and space, but in a particular sense, as dwelling in eternity: and therefore capable of beholding eternal realities, and coming into communion with absolute beauty, and goodness, and truth—that is, with God, the Absolute Being."

79. Hence we may perceive the reason why Ceres as well as Saturn was denominated a

legislative deity; and why illuminations were used in the celebration of the Saturnalia, as well as in the Eleusinian Mysteries.

80. When the person turns the back upon his higher faculties, and disregards the communications which he receives through them from the world of unseen realities, an oblivion ensues of their existence, and the person is next brought within the province and operation of lower and worldly ambitions, such as a love of power, passion for riches, sensual pleasure, etc. This is a descent, fall, or apostasy of the soul,—a separation from the sources of divine life and ravishment into the region of moral death.

In the *Phædrus*, in the allegory of the Chariot and Winged Steeds, Plato represents the lower or inferior part of man's nature as dragging the soul down to the earth, and subjecting it to the slavery of corporeal conditions. Out of these conditions there arise numerous evils, that disorder the mind and becloud the reason, for evil is inherent to the condition of finite and multiform being into which we have "fallen by our own fault." The present earthly life is a fall and a punishment. The soul is now dwelling in "the grave which we call the body." In its incorporate state, and previous to the discipline of education, the rational element is "asleep." "Life is more of a dream than a reality." Men are utterly the slaves of sense, the sport of phantoms and illusions. We now resemble those "captives chained in a subterraneous cave," so poetically described in the seventh book of *The Republic;* their backs are turned to the light, and consequently they see but the shadows of the objects which pass behind them, and "they attribute to these shadows a perfect reality." Their sojourn upon earth is thus a dark imprisonment in the body, a dreamy exile from their proper home."—*Cocker's Greek Philosophy.*

81. PORPHYRY: *Cave of the Nymphs.* In the later Greek, νυμφη signified a bride.

82. HOMER: *Hymn to Ceres.* "We were plucking the pleasant flowers, the beauteous crocus, and the Iris, and hyacinth, and the narcissus, which, like the crocus, the wide earth produced. I was plucking them with joy, when the earth yawned beneath, and out leaped the Strong King, the Many-Receiver, and went bearing me, grieving much, beneath the earth in his golden chariot, and I cried aloud."

83. *Manteis*, μαντεις, not ἱερεις. The term is more commonly translated prophets, and actually signifies persons gifted with divine insight, through being in an entheastic condition, called also *mania* or divine fury.

84. "The soul is a composite nature, is on one side linked to the eternal world, its essence being generated of that ineffable element which constitutes the real, the immutable, and the permanent. It is a beam of the eternal Sun, a spark of the Divinity, an emanation from God. On the other hand, it is linked to the phenomenal or sensible world, its emotive part being formed of that which is relative and phenomenal."—*Cocker.*

85. *Hymn to Ceres.* "For nine days did holy Demeter perambulate the earth .. and when the ninth shining morn had come, Hecate met her, bringing news."

Apuleius also explains that at the initiation into the Mysteries of Isis the candidate was enjoined to abstain from luxurious food for ten days, from the flesh of animals, and from wine.—*Golden Ass*, book xi. p. 239 (*Bohn*).

86. Only persons taking a view solely external will suppose the galaxy to be literally the milky belt of stars in the sky.

87. *Cave of the Nymphs.*

88. *Theology of Plato*, book vi.
89. The Moon typified the mother of gods and men. The soul descending into the lunar orb thus came near the scenes of earthly existence, where the life which is transmitted by generation has opportunity to involve it about.
90. The condition most unlike the former divine estate.
91. An orbicular figure symbolized the maternal, and a cone the masculine divine Energy.
92. PROCLUS: *Theology of Plato*, book vi. c. 10.
93. HOMER: *Hymn to Ceres*. "To her Metaneira gave a cup of sweet wine, but she refused it; but bade her to mix wheat and water with pounded pennyroyal. Having made the mixture, she gave it to the goddess."
94. Γυνη, *gune*, woman, from γουνος, *gounos*, Latin *cunnus*.
95. Uncandidness was more probably the fault of which Clement was guilty.
96. *Divine Legation of Moses*, book ii.
97. "The wisest and best men in the Pagan world are unanimous in this, that the Mysteries were instituted pure, and proposed the noblest ends by the worthiest means.
98. *Mysteries of the Egyptians, Chaldeans, and Assyrians*.
99. A golden serpent, an egg, and the phallus. The epopt looking upon these, was rapt with awe as contemplating in the symbols the deeper mysteries of all life, or being of a grosser temper, took a lascivious impression. Thus as a *seer*, he beheld with the eyes of sense or sentiment; and the real apocalypse was therefore that made to himself of his own moral life and character.—A. W.
100. "Exiled from the true home of the spirit, imprisoned in the body, disordered by passion, and beclouded by sense, the soul has yet longings after that state of perfect knowledge, and purity, and bliss, in which it was first created. Its affinities are still on high. It yearns for a higher and nobler form of life. It essays to rise, but its eye is darkened by sense, its wings are besmeared by passion and lust; it is 'borne downward until it falls upon and attaches itself to that which is material and sensual,' and it flounders and grovels still amid the objects of sense. And now, Plato asks: How may the soul be delivered from the illusions of sense, the distempering influence of the body, and the disturbances of passion, which becloud its vision of the real, the good, and the true?"
    "Plato believed and hoped that this could be accomplished by *philosophy*. This he regarded as a grand intellectual discipline for the purification of the soul. By this it was to be disenthralled from the bondage of sense, and raised into the empyrean of pure thought, 'where truth and reality shine forth.' All souls have the faculty of knowing, but it is only by reflection and self-knowledge, and intellectual discipline, that the soul can be raised to the vision of eternal truth, goodness, and beauty—that is, to the vision of God."—COCKER: *Christianity and Greek Philosophy*, x. pp. 351-2.
101. "It is linked to the phenomenal or sensible world, its emotive part (επιθυμητικον) being formed of what is relative and phenomenal."
102. KIRCHER: *Obeliscus Pamphilius*, page 227.
103. PLUTARCH: *Euseb.*
104. *I. e.* Exposition of the laws and operations of Nature.
105. Μυστηριωδης, mystery-like.

Psyche Asleep in Hades.

River Goddesses.

SECTION II.

The Bacchic Mysteries

THE DIONYSIACAL SACRED rites instituted by Orpheus, [106] depended on the following arcane narration, part of which has been already related in the preceding section, and the rest may be found in a variety of authors. "Dionysus, or Bacchus [Zagreus], while he was yet a boy, was engaged by the Titans, through the stratagems of Juno, in a variety of sports, with which that period of life is so vehemently allured; and among the rest, he was particularly captivated with beholding his image in a mirror; during his admiration of which, he was miserably torn in pieces by the Titans; who, not content with this cruelty, first boiled his members in water, and afterwards roasted them by the fire. But while they were tasting his flesh thus dressed, Jupiter, roused by the odor, and perceiving the cruelty of the deed, hurled his thunder at the Titans; but committed the members of Bacchus to Apollo, his brother, that they might be properly interred. And this being performed, Dionysus (whose heart during his laceration was snatched away by Pallas and preserved), by a new regeneration again emerged, and being restored to his pristine life and integrity, he afterwards filled up the number of the gods. But in the mean time, from the exhalations arising from the ashes of the burning bodies of the Titans, mankind were produced." Now, in order to understand properly the secret of this narration, it is necessary to repeat the observation already made in the preceding chapter, "that all fables belonging to mystic ceremonies are of the mixed kind": and consequently the present fable, as well as that of Proserpina, must in one part have reference to the gods, and in the other to the human soul, as the following exposition will abundantly evince:

In the first place, then, by Dionysus, or Bacchus, according to the highest conception of this deity, we understand the spiritual part of the mundane soul; for there are various processions or avatars of this god, or Bacchuses, derived from his essence. But by the Titans we must understand the mundane gods, of whom Bacchus is the highest; by Jupiter, the Demiurgus, [107] or artificer of the universe; by Apollo, the deity of the Sun, who has both a mundane and super-mundane establishment, and by whom the universe is bound in symmetry and consent, through splendid reasons and harmonizing power; and, lastly, by Minerva we must understand that original, intellectual, ruling, and providential deity, who guards and preserves all middle lives [108] in an immutable condition, through intelligence and a self-supporting life, and by this means sustains them from the depredations and inroads of matter. Again, by the infancy of Bacchus at the period of his laceration, the condition of the intellectual nature is implied; since, according to the Orphic theology, souls, under the government of Saturn, or Kronos, who is pure intellect or spirituality, instead of proceeding, as now, from youth to age, advance in a retrograde progression from age to youth. [109] The arts employed by the Titans, in order to ensnare Dionysius, are symbolical of those apparent and divisible energies of the mundane gods, through which the participated intellect of Bacchus becomes, as it were, torn in pieces; and by the mirror we must understand, in the language of Proclus, the inaptitude of the universe to receive the plenitude of intellectual perfection; but the symbolical meaning of his laceration, through the stratagems of Juno, and the consequent punishment of the Titans, is thus beautifully unfolded by Olympiodorus, in his MS. Commentary on the *Phædo* of Plato: "The form," says he, "of that which is universal is plucked off, torn in pieces, and scattered into generation; and Dionysus is the *monad* of the Titans. But his laceration is said to take place through the stratagems of Juno, because this goddess is the supervising guardian of motion and progression; [110] and on this account, in the *Iliad*, she perpetually rouses and excites Jupiter to providential action about secondary concerns; and, in another respect, Dionysus is the *ephorus* or supervising guardian of generation, because he presides over life and death; for he is the guardian or *ephorus* of life because of generation, and also of death because wine produces an enthusiastic condition. We become more enthusiastic at the period of dying, as Proclus indicates in the example of Homer who became prophetic [μαντικος] at the time of his death. [111] They likewise assert, that tragedy and comedy are assigned to Dionysus: comedy being the play or ludicrous representation of life; and tragedy having relation to the *passions* and *death*. The comic writers, therefore, do not rightly call in question the tragedians as not rightly representing Bacchus, saying that such things did not happen to

Bacchus. But Jupiter is said to have hurled his thunder at the Titans; the thunder signifying a conversion or changing: for fire naturally ascends; and hence Jupiter, by this means, converts the Titans to his own essence." Σπαραττεται δε το καθολου ειδος εν τη γενεσει, μονας δε Τιτανων ὁ Διονυσος.–Κατ᾽ επιβουλην δε της Ἡρας διοτι κινησεως εφορος ἡ θεος και προοδου. Διο και συνεχως εν τη Ιλιασι εξανιστησιν αυτη, και διεγορει τον δια εις προνοιαν των δευτερων. Και γενεσεως αλλως εφορος εστιν ὁ Διονυσος, διοτι και ζωης και τελευτης. Ζωης μεν γαρ εφορος, επειδη και της γενεσεως, τελευτης δε διοτι ενθουσιαν ὁ οινος ποιει. Και περι την τελευτην δε ενθουσιαστικωτεροι γινομεθα, ὡς δηλοι ὁ παρ᾽ Ὁμηρῳ Προκλος, μαντικος γεγονως περι την τελευτην· και την τραγωδιαν, και την κωμωδιαν ανεισθαι φασι τῳ Διονυσῳ. Την μεν κωμωδιαν παιγνιον ουσαν του βιον· την δε τραγωδιαν δια τα παθη, και την τελευτην. Ουκ αρα καλως οἱ κωμικοι τοις τραγικοις εγκαλουσιν, ὡς μη Διονυσιακοις ουσιν, λεγον τες οτι ουδεν ταυτα προς τον Διονυσον. Κεραυνοι δε τουτοις ὁ Ζευς, του κεραυνου δηλουντος την επιστροφεν· πυργαρ επι τα ανω κινουμενα· επιστρεφει ουν αυτους προς εαυτον.

But by the members of Dionysus being first boiled in water by the Titans, and afterward roasted by the fire, the outgoing or distribution of intellect into matter, and its subsequent returning from thence, is evidently implied: for water was considered by the Egyptians, as we have already observed, as the symbol of matter; and fire is the natural symbol of ascending. The heart of Dionysus too, is, with the greatest propriety, said to be preserved by Minerva; for this goddess is the guardian of life, of which the heart is a symbol. So that this part of the fable plainly signifies, that while intellectual or spiritual life is distributed into the universe, its principle is preserved entire by the guardian power and providence of the Divine intelligence. And as Apollo is the source of all union and harmony, and as he is called by Proclus, "the key-keeper of the fountain of life," [112] the reason is obvious why the members of Dionysus, which were buried by this deity, again emerged by a new generation, and were restored to their pristine integrity and life. But let it here be carefully observed, that renovation, when applied to the gods, is to be considered as secretly implying the rising of their proper light, and its consequent appearance to subordinate natures. And that punishment, when considered as taking place about beings of a nature superior to mankind, signifies nothing more than a secondary providence over such beings which is of a punishing character, and which subsists about souls that deteriorate. Hence, then, from what has been said, we may easily collect the ultimate design of the first part of this mystic fable; for it appears to be no other than to represent the manner in which the form of the mundane intellect is divided through the universe;—that such an intellect (and every one which is total) remains entire during its division into parts, and that the divided parts themselves are continually turned again to their source, with which they become finally united. So that illumination from the higher reason, while it proceeds into the dark and rebounding receptacle of matter, and invests its obscurity with the supervening ornaments of divine light, returns at the same time without interruption to the source or principle of its descent.

Etruscan Eleusinians.

SECTION II. The Bacchic Mysteries

Let us now consider the latter part of the fable, in which it is said that our souls were formed from the vapors emanating from the ashes of the burning bodies of the Titans; at the same time connecting it with the former part of the fable, which is also applicable in a certain degree to the condition of a partial intellect [113] like ours. In the first place, then, we are made up from *fragments* (says Olympiodorus), because, through falling into generation, our life has proceeded into the most distant and extreme division; and from *Titanic fragments*, because the Titans are the ultimate artificers of things, [114] and stand immediately next to whatever is constituted from them. But further, our irrational life is Titanic, by which the rational and higher life is torn in pieces. Hence, when we disperse the Dionysus, or intuitive intellect contained in the secret recesses of our nature, breaking in pieces the kindred and divine form of our essence, and which communicates, as it were, both with things subordinate and supreme, then we become Titans (or apostates); but when we establish ourselves in union with this Dionysiacal or kindred form, then we become Bacchuses, or perfect guardians and keepers of our irrational life: for Dionysus, whom in this respect we resemble, is himself an *ephorus* or guardian deity, dissolving at his pleasure the bonds by which the soul is united to the body, since he is the cause of a parted life. But it is necessary that the passive or feminine nature of our irrational part, through which we are bound in body, and which is nothing more than the resounding echo, as it were, of soul, should suffer the punishment incurred by descent; for when the soul casts aside the [divine] peculiarity of her nature, she requires her own, but at the same time a multiform body, that she may again become in need of a common form, which she has lost through Titanic dispersion into matter.

But in order to see the perfect resemblance between the manner in which our souls descend and the dividing of the intuitive intellect by mundane natures, let the reader attend to the following admirable citation from the manuscript Commentary of Olympiodorus on the *Phædo* of Plato: "It is necessary, first of all, for the soul to place a likeness of herself in the body. This is to ensoul the body. Secondly, it is necessary for her to sympathize with the image, as being of like idea. For every external form or substance is wrought into an identity with its interior substance, through an ingenerated tendency thereto. In the third place, being situated in a divided nature, it is necessary that she should be torn in pieces, and fall into a last separation, till, through the action of a life of purification, she shall raise herself from the dispersion, loose the bond of sympathy, and act as of herself without the external image, having become established according to the first-created life. The like things are fabled in the example. For Dionysus or Bacchus because his image was formed in a mirror, pursued it, and thus became distributed into everything. But Apollo collected him and brought him up; being a deity of purification, and the true savior of Dionysus; and on this account he is styled in the sacred hymns, Dionusites." Ότι δει πρωτον ὑποστησαι εκονα την ψυχην εαυτου εν τῳ σωματι. Τουτο γαρ εστι ψυχωσαι το σωμα. Δευτερον δε συμπαθειν τῳ ειδωλῳ, κατα την ὁμοειδειαν. Παν γαρ ειδος επειγεται εις την προς εαυτο ταυτοητα δια την προς εαυτο συνευσιν εμφυτον. Τριτον εν τῳ μερισμῳ γενομενην συνδιαπασθηναι αυτῳ, και εις τον εσχατον εκπεσειν μερισμον. Έως αν δαι της καθαρτιηκης ζωης συναγειραι μεν έαυτην απο του σκορπισμου, λυση δε τον δεσμον της συμηπαθειας, προβαλλεται δε την ανευ του ειδωλου, καθ' εαυτην έστωσαν πρωτουργον ζωην. Ότι τα όμοια μυθευεται, και εν τω παραδειγματι. Ὁ γαρ Διονυσος, ότι το ειδωλον ενεθηκε τω εσοπτρω τουτω εφεσπετο. Και όυτως εις το παν εμερισθη. Ὁ δε Απολλων συναγειρει τε αυτον και αναγει, καθαρτικος ων θεος, και του Διονυσου σωτηρ ως αλφθως. Και δια τουτο Διονυσοτης ανυμειται. Hence, as the same author beautifully observes, the soul revolves according to a mystic and mundane revolution: for flying from an indivisible and Dionysiacal life, and operating according to a Titanic and revolting energy, she becomes bound in the body as in a prison. Hence, too, she abides in punishment and takes care of her partial and secondary concerns; and being purified from Titanic defilements, and collected into one, she becomes a Bacchus; that is, she passes into the proper integrity of her nature according to the divine principle ruling on high. From all which it evidently follows, that he who lives Dionysiacally rests from labors and is freed from his bonds; [115] that he leaves his prison, or rather his apostatizing life; and that he who does this is a philosopher purifying himself from the contaminations of his earthly life. But farther from this account of Dionysus, we may perceive the truth of Plato's observation, "that the design of the Mysteries is to lead us back to the perfection from which, as our beginning, we first made our descent." For in this perfection Dionysus himself subsists, establishing perfect souls in the throne of his father; that is, in the integrity of a life according to Jupiter. So that he who is perfect necessarily resides with the gods, according to the design of those deities, who are the sources of consummate perfection to the soul. And lastly, the Thyrsus itself, which was used in the Bacchic procession, as it was a reed full of knots, is an apt symbol of the diffusion of the higher nature into the sensible world. And agreeable to this, Olympiodorus on the *Phædo* observes, "that the Thyrsus [116] is a symbol of a forming anew of the material and parted substance from its scattered condition; and that on this account it is a Titanic plant. This it was customary to extend before Bacchus instead of his paternal scepter; and through this they called him down into our partial nature. Indeed, the Titans are Thyrsus-bearers; and Prometheus concealed fire in a Thyrus or reed; after which he is considered as bringing celestial light into generation, or leading the soul into the body, or calling forth the divine illumination, the whole being ungenerated, into generated existence. Hence Socrates calls the multitude Thyrsus-bearers Orphically, as living according to a Titanic life." Ὅτι ὁ ναρθηξ συμβολον εστι της ενυλου δημιουργιας, και μεριστης, δια την μαλιστα διεσπαρμενην συνεχειαν, οθεν και Τιτανικον το φυτον. Και γαρ τῳ Διονυσῳ προτεινουσιν αυτῳ, αντι του πατρικου σκηπτρου. Και ταυτη προκαλουνται αυτον εις τον μερικον. Και μεντοι, και ναρθηκοφορουσιν οἱ Τιτανες, και ὁ Προμηθευς, εν ναρθηκϊ κλεπτι το πυρ, ειτε το ουρανιον φως εις την γενεσιν κατασπων, ειτε την ψυχην εις το σωμα προαγων, ειτε την θειαν ελλαμψιν ὁλην αγεννητον ουσαν, εις την γενεσιν προκαλουμενος. Δια δε τουτο, και ὁ Σωκρατης τους πολλους καλει ναρθηκοφορους Ορφικως, ὡς ζωντας Τιτανικως.

Faun and Bacchante. Thyrsus-Bearer. Bacchante and Faun.

And thus much for the secret meaning of the fable, which formed a principal part of these mystic rites. Let us now proceed to consider the signification of the symbols, which, according to Clemens Alexandrinus, belonged to the Bacchic ceremonies; and which are comprehended in the following Orphic verses:

Κωνος, και ρομβος, και παιγνια καμπεσιγυια
Μηλα τε χρυσεα καλα παρ ἑσπεριδων λιγυφωνων.

That is,

A wheel, a pine-nut, and the wanton plays,
Which move and bend the limbs in various ways:
With these th' Hesperian golden-fruit combine,
Which beauteous nymphs defend of voice divine.

To all which Clemens adds εσοπτρον, *esoptron, a mirror,* ποκος, *pokos, a fleece of wool,* and αστραγαλος, *astragalos, the ankle-bone.*

In the first place, then, with respect to the wheel, since Dionysus, as we have already explained, is the mundane intellect, and intellect is of an elevating and convertive nature, nothing can be a more apt symbol of intellectual action than a wheel or sphere: besides, as the laceration and dismemberment of Dionysus signifies the going-forth of intellectual illumination into matter, and its returning at the same time to its source, this too will be aptly symbolized by a wheel. In the second place, a *pine-nut, from its conical shape*, is a perspicuous symbol of the manner in which intellectual or spiritual illumination proceeds from its source and beginning into a material nature. "For the soul," says Macrobius, [117] "proceeding from a round figure, which is the only divine form, is extended into the form of a cone in going forth." And the same is true symbolically of the higher intellect. And as to the wanton sports which bend the limbs, this evidently alludes to the Titanic arts, by which Dionysus was allured, and occultly signifies the faculties of the mundane intellect, considered as subsisting according to an apparent and divisible condition. But the Hesperian golden-apples signify the pure and incorruptible nature of that intellect or Dionysus, which is possessed by the world; for a golden-apple, according to Sallust, is a symbol of the world; and this doubtless, both on account of its external figure, and the incorruptible intellect which it contains, and with the illuminations of which it is externally adorned; since gold, on account of never being subject to rust, aptly denotes an incorruptible and immaterial nature. The mirror, which is the next symbol, we have already explained. And as to the fleece of wool, this is a symbol of laceration, or distribution of intellect, or Dionysus, into matter; for the verb σπαραττω, *sparatto, dilanio*, which is used in the relation of the Bacchic discerption, signifies to tear in pieces like wool: and hence Isidorus derives the Latin word *lana, wool*, from *laniando*, as *vellus* from *vellendo*. Nor must it pass unobserved, that λῆνος, in Greek, signifies wool, and ληνὸς, a wine-press. [118] And, indeed, the pressing of grapes is as evident a symbol of dispersion as the tearing of wool; and this circumstance was doubtless one principal reason why grapes were consecrated to Bacchus: for a grape, previous to its pressure, aptly represents that which is collected into one; and when it is pressed into juice, it no less aptly represents the diffusion of that which was before collected and entire. And lastly, the αστραγαλος, *astragalos*, or *ankle-bone*, as it is principally subservient to the progressive motion of animals, so it belongs, with great propriety, to the mystic symbols of Bacchus; since it doubtless signifies the going forth of that deity into the department of physical existence: for nature, or that divisible life which subsists about the body, and which is productive of seeds, immediately depends on Bacchus. And hence we are informed by Proclus, that the sexual parts of this god are denominated by theologists, *Diana*, who, says he, presides over the whole of the generation into natural existence, leads forth into light all natural reasons, and extends a prolific power from on high even to the subterranean realms. [119] And hence we may perceive the reason why, in the Orphic *Hymn to Nature*, that goddess is described as "*turning round silent traces with the* ankle-bones *of her feet.*"

Αψοφον αστραγαλοισι ποδων ιχνος ειλισσουσα.

Hercules Reclining.

SECTION II. The Bacchic Mysteries

And it is highly worthy our observation that in this verse of the hymn Nature is celebrated as Fortune, according to that description of the goddess in which she is represented as standing with her feet on a wheel which she continually turns round; as the following verse from the same hymn abundantly confirms:

Αεναῳ στροφαλιγγι θοον ῥυμα δινευουσα.

The sense of which is, "moving with rapid motion on an eternal wheel." Nor ought it to seem wonderful that Nature should he celebrated as Fortune; for Fortune in the Orphic hymn to that deity is invoked as Diana: and the moon, as we have observed in the preceding section, is the αυτοπτον αγαλμα φυσεως, *the self-revealing emblem of Nature;* and indeed the apparent inconstancy of Fortune has an evident agreement with the fluctuating condition in which the dominions of nature are perpetually involved.

It only now remains that we explain the secret meaning of the sacred dress with which the initiated in the Dionysiacal Mysteries were invested, in order to the θρονισμος (*thronismos,* enthroning) taking place; or sitting in a solemn manner on a throne, about which it was customary for the other initiates to dance. But the particulars of this habit are thus described in the Orphic verses preserved by Macrobius: [120]

Ταυτα γε παντα τελειν ιερα σκηυῃ πυκασαντα,
Σωμα θεου πλαττειν εριαυγους ἠελιοιο.
Πρωτα μεν αργυφεαις εναλιγκιον ακτινεσσιν

Πεπλον φοινικερον (lege φοινικεον) πρυῖικελον αμφιβαλεσθαι.
Αυταρ ύπερθε νεβροιο παναιολου είρυ καθαψαι
Δερμα πολυστικτον θηρος κατα δεξιον ὡμον,
Αστρων δαιδαλεων μιμιμ' ίερου τε πολοιο.
Είτα δ' ύπερθε νεβρης χρυσεον ζωστηρα βαλεσθαι
Παμφανοωντα περιξ στερνων φορεειν μεγα σημα
Ευθυς ότ' εκ περατων Γαιης φαεθων ανορουσων
Χρυσειαις ακτισι βαλη ροον Οκεανοιο,
Αυγη δ' άσπετος ή, ανα δ' δροσῳ αμφιμιγεισα
Μαρμαιρη δινησιν ελισσομενη κατα κυκλον,
Προσθε θεου. Ζωνη δ' αρ ύπο στερνων αμετρητων
Φαινετ' αρ' Ωκεανου κυκλος, μεγα θαυμ' εισιδεσθαι.

That is,

He who desires in pomp of sacred dress
The sun's resplendent body to express,
Should first a vail assume of purple bright,
Like fair white beams combin'd with fiery light:
On his right shoulder, next, a mule's broad hide
Widely diversified with spotted pride
Should hang, an image of the pole divine,
And dædal stars, whose orbs eternal shine.
A golden splendid zone, then, o'er the vest
He next should throw, and bind it round his breast;
In mighty token, how with golden light,
The rising sun, from earth's last bounds and night

Sudden emerges, and, with matchless force,
Darts through old Ocean's billows in his course.
A boundless splendor hence, enshrin'd in dew,
Plays on his whirlpools, glorious to the view;
While his circumfluent waters spread abroad,
Full in the presence of the radiant god:
But Ocean's circle, like a zone of light,
The sun's wide bosom girds, and charms the wond'ring sight.

In the first place, then, let us consider why this mystic dress belonging to Bacchus is to represent the sun. Now the reason of this will be evident from the following observations: according to the Orphic theology, the divine intellect of every planet is denominated a Bacchus, who is characterized in each by a different appellation; so that the intellect of the solar deity is called Trietericus Bacchus. And in the second place, since the divinity of the sun, according to the arcana of the ancient theology, has a super-mundane as well as mundane establishment, and is wholly of an exalting or intellectual nature; hence considered as super-mundane he must both produce and contain the mundane intellect, or Dionysus, in his essence; for all the mundane are contained in the super-mundane deities, by whom also they are produced. Hence Proclus, in his elegant *Hymn to the Sun*, says:

Σε κλυτον ὑμνειουσι Διωνυσσοιο τοκηα.

That is, "they celebrate thee in hymns as the illustrious parent of Dionysus." And thirdly, it is through the subsistence of Dionysus in the sun that that luminary derives its circular motion, as is evident from the following Orphic verse, in which, speaking of the sun, it is said of him, that

–Διονυσος δ' επεκληθη,
Ουνεκα δινειται κατ' απειρονα μακρον Ολυμπον.

"He is called Dionysus, because he is carried with a circular motion through the immensely-extended heavens." And this with the greatest propriety, since intellect, as we have already observed, is entirely of a transforming and elevating nature: so that from all this, it is sufficiently evident why the dress of Dionysus is represented as belonging to the sun. In the second place, the vail, resembling a mixture of fiery light, is an obvious image of the solar fire. And as to the spotted mule-skin, [121] which is to represent the starry heavens, this is nothing more than an image of the moon; this luminary, according to Proclus *on Hesiod*, resembling the mixed nature of a mule; "becoming dark through her participation of earth, and deriving her proper light from the sun." Γης μεν εχουσα το σκοτιζεσθαι, ήλιου δε το οικειον ειληχεναι φως. Ταυτη μεν ουν οικειωται προς αυτην ή ήμιονος. So that the spotted hide signifies the moon attended with a multitude of stars: and hence, in the Orphic *Hymn to the Moon*, that deity is celebrated "as shining surrounded with beautiful stars": καλοις αστροισι βρυουσα, and is likewise called αστραρχη, *astrarché*, or *"queen of the stars."*

The Marriage of Mars and Venus.

In the next place, the golden zone is the circle of the Ocean, as the last verses plainly evince. But, you will ask, what has the rising of the sun through the ocean, from the boundaries of earth and night, to do with the adventures of Bacchus? I answer, that it is inpossible to devise a symbol more beautifully accommodated to the purpose: for, in the first place, is not the ocean a proper emblem of an earthly nature, whirling and stormy, and perpetually rolling without admitting any periods of repose? And is not the sun emerging from its boisterous deeps a perspicuous symbol of the higher spiritual nature, apparently rising from the dark and fluctuating material receptacle, and conferring form and beauty on the sensible universe through its light? I say apparently rising, for though the spiritual nature always diffuses its splendor with invariable energy, yet it is not always perceived by the subjects of its illuminations: besides, as psychical natures can only receive partially and at intervals the benefits of the divine irradiation; hence fables regarding this temporal participation transfer, for the purpose of concealment and in conformity to the phenomena, the imperfection of subordinate natures to such as are supreme. This description, therefore, of the rising sun, is a most beautiful symbol of the new birth of Bacchus, which, as we have already observed, implies nothing more than the rising of intellectual light, and its consequent manifestation to subordinate orders of existence.

And thus much for the mysteries of Bacchus, which, as well as those of Ceres, relate in one part to the descent of a partial intellect into matter, and its condition while united with the dark tenement of the body: but there appears to be this difference between the two, that in the fable of Ceres and Proserpine the descent of the whole rational soul is considered; and in that of Bacchus the scattering and going forth of *that supreme part alone of our nature which we properly characterize by the appellation of intellect.* [122] In the composition of each we may discern the same traces of exalted wisdom and recondite theology; of a theology the most venerable for its antiquity, and the most admirable for its excellence and reality.

I shall conclude this treatise by presenting the reader with a valuable and most elegant hymn of Proclus [123] to Minerva, which I have discovered in the British Museum; and the existence of which appears to have been hitherto utterly unknown. This hymn is to be found among the Harleian Manuscripts, in a volume containing several of the *Orphic hymns*, with which, through the ignorance of transcriber, it is indiscriminately ranked, as well as the other four hymns of Proclus, already printed in the *Bibliotheca Græca* of Fabricius. Unfortunately too, it is transcribed in a character so obscure. and with such great inaccuracy, that, notwithstanding the pains I have taken to restore the text to its original purity, I have been obliged to omit two lines, and part of a third, as beyond my abilities to read or amend; however, the greatest, and doubtless the most important part, is fortunately intelligible, which I now present to the reader's inspection, accompanied with some corrections, and an English paraphrased translation. The original is highly elegant and pious, and contains one mythological particular, which is no where else to be found. It has likewise an evident connection with the preceding fable of Bacchus, as will be obvious from the perusal; and on this account principally it was inserted in the present discourse.

FOOTNOTES

106. Whether Orpheus was an actual living person has been questioned by Aristotle; but Herodotus, Pindar, and other writers, mention him. Although the Orphic system is asserted to have come from Egypt, the internal evidence favors the opinion that it was derived from India, and that its basis is the Buddhistic philosophy. The Orphic associations of Greece were ascetic, contrasting markedly with the frenzies, enthusiasm, and license of the popular rites. The Thracians had numerous Hindu customs. The name Koré is Sanscrit; and Zeus may be the Dyaus of Hindu story. His visit to the chamber of Koré-Persephoneia (Parasu-pani) in the form of a dragon or *naga*, and the horns or crescent on the head of the child, are Tartar or Buddhistic. The name Zagreus is evidently *Chakra*, or ruler of the earth. The *Hera* who compassed his death is *Aira*, the wife of Buddha; and the Titans are the Daityas, or apostate tribes of India. The doctrine of metempsychosis is expressed by the swallowing of the heart of the murdered child, so as to reabsorb his soul, and bring him anew into existence as the son of Semelé. Indeed, all the stories of Bacchus have Hindu characteristics; and his cultus is a part of the serpent worship of the ancients. The evidence appears to us unequivocal. A. W.

107. Plotinus regarded the Demiurgus, or creator, as the god of providence, thought, essence, and power. Above him was the deity of "pure intellect," and still higher The One. These three were the hypostases.

108. Lives which are not conjoined with material bodies, nor yet elevated to the lofty state which is the true divine condition.

109. Emanuel Swedenborg says: "They who are in heaven are continually advancing to the spring of life, and the more thousands of years they live, so much the more delightful and happy is the spring to which they attain, and this to eternity with increments according to the progresses and degrees of love, of charity, and of faith. Women who have died old and worn out with age, yet have lived in faith on the Lord, in charity toward their neighbor, and in happy conjugal love with a husband, after a succession of years, come more and more into the flower of youth and adolescence."

110. By progression [πρoοδος] is here signified the raying-out, or issuing forth of the soul; having left the divine or pre-existent life, and come forth toward the human.

111. See also PLATO: *Phædrus*, 43. "When I was about to cross the river, the divine and wonted signal was given me—it always deters me from what I am about to do—and I seemed to hear a voice from this very spot, which would not suffer me to depart before I had purified myself, as if I had committed some offense against the Deity. Now I am a prophet, though not a very good one: for the soul is in some measure prophetic."
See also SHAKSPERE: *Henry IV*. part 1.
"Oh I could prophesy,
But that the earthy and cold hand of death
Lies on my tongue."

112. *Hymn to the Sun.*

113. Partial, as being parted from the Supreme Mind.

114. The Demiurge or Creator being superior to matter in which is concupiscence and all evil, the Titans who are not thus superior are made the actual artificers.

115. "We strive toward virtue by a strenuous use of the gifts which God communicates; but when God communicates himself, then we can be only passive—we repose, we enjoy,

but all operation ceases."

116. The word thyrsus, it will be seen, is here translated from ναρθηξ, a rod or feru a.
117. *In Somnia Scipionis*, xii.
118. The practice of punning, so common in all the old rites, is here forcibly exhibited. It aided to conceal the symbolism and mislead uninitiated persons who might seek to ascertain the genuine meaning.
119. *Commentary upon the Timæus*.
120. *Saturnalia*, i. 18.
121. *Nebris* is also a fawn-skin. The Jewish high-priest wore one at the great festivals. It is rendered "badger's skin" in the Bible. In India the robe of Indra is spotted.
122. Greek, νους, *nous*, the Intuitive Reason, that faculty of the mind that apprehends the Ineffable Truth.
123. That the following hymn was composed by Proclus, can not be doubted by any one who is conversant with those already extant of this incomparable man, since the spirit and manner in both is perfectly the same.

Hymn to Minerva

Εις ΑΘΗΝΑΝ

ΚΛΥΘΙ μευ αιγιοχοιο διος τεκος· ή γενετηρος
Πηγης εκπροθορουσα, και ακροτατης απο σειρας
Αρσενοθυμε· φερασπι· μεγασθενες· οβριμοπατηρ, [124]
Κεκλυθι· δεχνυσο δ' ύμνον ευφρονι ποτνια θυμω
Ή σοφιης πετασασα θεοστυβεας [125] πυλεωνας.
Και χθονιων δαμασασα θεωμαχα φυλα γιγαντων.
Ή κραδιην εσαωσας αμυστιλευτον [126] ανακτος
Αιθερος εν γυαλοισι μεριζομενου ποτε Βακχου
Τιτανων ύπο χερσι, πορες δε ε πατρι φερουσα
Οφρα νεος βουλησιν απ' αρρητοισι τοκηος,
Εκ Σεμελης περι κοσμον ανηβηση Διονυσσος.
Ής πελεκις [127] θηριων ταμνων προθελυμνα καρηνα
Πανδερκους έκατης παθεων ήνυσε γενεθλην·
Ή κρατος Ήρας σεμνον εγερσι βροτων αρετα·ων
Η βιοτον κοσμησας ολον πολυειδεσι τεχναις,
Δεμιουργικην οερην [128] ψυχαισι βαλλουσα·
Ή λαχες αχροπολια . . . . . .
Συμβολον ακροτατης μεγαλης σεο ποτνια σειρης·
Ή χθονα βωτιανειρα φιλησας μητερας βιβλων.
Ουνομα αστυ δε δωκας εχειν σεο και φρενας εσθλας.
Κλυθι μευ ή φαος άγνον απαστραπτουσα προσωπου·
Δος δε μοι ολβιον ορμον άλωμενα περι γαιαν.

Δος ψυχῃ φαος αγνον απ᾽ ευιρεων σεο μυθων·

Και σοφιην· και ερωτα· μενος δ᾽ εμπνευσον ερωτι,

Τοσσατιον, και τοιον, οσον χθονιων απο κολπων

Αψερνη προς Ολυμπον ες ηθεα πατροσ εοιο,

Ειδε τις αμπλακιημε [129] κακη βιοτοιο δαμαζει.

Ιλαθι μειλιχοβουλε· σαομβρστε· μηδεμεασης [130]

῾Ριγεδαναις ποιναισιν ελωρ και κυρμα γενεσσα,

Κειμενον εν δαπεδοισιν, ότι τεος ευχομαι ειναι·

Κεκλυθι κεκλυθι· και μοι μειλισχιν ουας ὑποχες.

To Minerva

Daughter of ægis-bearing Jove, divine,
Propitious to thy votaries' prayer incline;
From thy great father's fount supremely bright,
Like fire resounding, leaping into light.
Shield-bearing goddess, hear, to whom belong
A manly mind, and power to tame the strong!
Oh, sprung from matchless might, with joyful mind
Accept this hymn; benevolent and kind!
The holy gates of wisdom, by thy hand
Are wide unfolded; and the daring band
Of earth-born giants, that in impious fight
Strove with thy fire, were vanquished by thy might.
Once by thy care, as sacred poets sing,
The heart of Bacchus, swiftly-slaughtered king,
Was sav'd in Æther, when, with fury fired,
The Titans fell against his life conspired;
And with relentless rage and thirst for gore,
Their hands his members into fragments tore:
But ever watchful of thy father's will,
Thy power preserv'd him from succeeding ill,
Till from the secret counsels of his fire,
And born from Semelé through heavenly sire,
Great Dionysus to the world at length
Again appeared with renovated strength.
Once, too, thy warlike ax, with matchless sway,

Lopped from their savage necks the heads away
Of furious beasts, and thus the pests destroyed
Which long all-seeing Hecaté annoyed.
By thee benevolent great Juno's might
Was roused, to furnish mortals with delight.
And thro' life's wide and various range, 't is thine
Each part to beautify with art divine:
Invigorated hence by thee, we find
A demiurgic impulse in the mind.
Towers proudly raised, and for protection strong,
To thee, dread guardian deity, belong,
As proper symbols of th' exalted height
Thy series claims amidst the courts of light.
Lands are beloved by thee, to learning prone,
And Athens, Oh Athena, is thy own!
Great goddess, hear! and on my dark'ned mind
Pour thy pure light in measure unconfined;—
That sacred light, Oh all-protecting queen,
Which beams eternal from thy face serene.
My soul, while wand'ring on the earth, inspire
With thy own blessed and impulsive fire:
And from thy fables, mystic and divine,
Give all her powers with holy light to shine.
Give love, give wisdom, and a power to love,
Incessant tending to the realms above;
Such as unconscious of base earth's control
Gently attracts the vice-subduing soul:

From night's dark region aids her to retire,
And once more gain the palace of her sire.
O all-propitious to my prayer incline!
Nor let those horrid punishments be mine
Which guilty souls in Tartarus confine,
With fetters fast'ned to its brazen floors,
And lock'd by hell's tremendous iron doors.
Hear me, and save (for power is all thine own)
A soul desirous to be thine alone. [131]

It is very remarkable in this hymn, that the exploits of Minerva relative to cutting off the heads of wild beasts with an ax, etc., is mentioned by no writer whatever; nor can I find the least trace of a circumstance either in the history of Minerva or Hecate to which it alludes. [132] And from hence, I think, we may reasonably conclude that it belonged to the arcane Orphic narrations concerning these goddesses, which were consequently but rarely mentioned, and this but by a few, whose works, which might afford us some clearer information, are unfortunately lost.

FOOTNOTES

124. Lege οβριμοπατρη.
125. Lege θεοσεβειας.
126. Lege αμυσι λυτου.
127. Lege πελεκυς.
128. Lege Ορμην.
129. Lege αμπλακημα.
130. Lege μηδ' εμ' εασης.
131. If I should ever be able to publish a second edition of my translation of the hymns of Orpheus, I shall add to it a translation of all those hymns of Proclus, which are fortunately extant; but which are nothing more than the wreck of a great multitude which he composed.
132. If Mr. Taylor had been conversant with Hindu literature, he would have perceived that these exploits of Minerva-Athenè were taken from the buffalo-sacrifice of Durga or Bhavani. The whole Dionysiac legend is but a rendering of the Sivaic and Buddhistic legends into a Grecian dress.—A. W.

Musical Conference.

Appendix

Venus Rising from the Sea.

SINCE WRITING THE above Dissertation, I have met with a curious Greek manuscript entitled: "Of Psellus, *Concerning Dæmons,* [133] *according to the opinion of the Greeks"*: του Ψελλου τινα περι δαιμονων δοξαζουσιν Ελληνες: In the course of which he describes the machinery of the Eleusinian Mysteries as follows:—Ἁ δε γε μυστηρια τουτων, οἰον αυτικα τα Ελευσινια, τον μυθικον ὑποκρινεται δια μιγνυμενον τη δηοι, ἠ τη Δημητερι, και τη Θυγατερει ταυτης Φερσεφαττη τη και Κορη. Επειδη δε εμελλον και αφροδισιοι επι τη μυησει γινεσθαι συμπλοκαι, αναδυεται πως ἡ Αφροδιτη απο τινων πεπλασμενων μηδεων τελαγιος. Ειτα δε γαμηλιος επι τη Κορη ὑμεναιος. Και επαδουσιν οἱ τελουμενοι, εκ τυμπανου εφαγον εκ κυμβαλων επιον, εκιρνοφορησα (lege εκερνοφορησα) ὑπο τον παστον εισεδυν. Ὑποκρινεται δε και τας δηους ὠδινας. Ἱκετηριαι γουν αυτικα δηους. Και χολης ποσις, και καρδιαλγιαι. Εφ' οἱς και τραγοσκελες μιμημα παθαινομενον περι τοις διδυμοις· ὁτι περ ὁ Ζευς δικας αποτιννυς της βιας τη Δημητερι τεραγου (lege τραγου) ορχεις αποτεμων, τω κολπω ταυτης κατεθετο, ώσπερ δη και εαυτου. Επι πασιν αί του Διονυσου τιμαι, και ή κυστις, και τα πολυομφαλα ποπανα, και οί τω Σαβαζιω τελουμενοι, κληδονες τε και μιμαλωνες, και τις ηχων λεβης Θεσπρωτειος και Δωδωναιον χαλκειον, και Κορυβας αλλος και κουρης ετερος, δαιμονων μιμηματα. Εφ' οίς ή Βαβωτους (lege ή Βαυβω τους) μηρους ανασυρομενη, και ό γυναικος κτεις, ουτω γαρ ονομαζουσι την αιδω αισχυνομενοι. Και ουτως εν αισχρω την τελετην καταλυουσιν.

I. e. "The Mysteries of these demons, such as the Eleusinia, consisted in representing the mythical narration of Jupiter mingling with Ceres and her daughter Proserpina (Phersephatté). But as venereal connections are in the initiation, [134] a Venus is represented rising from the sea, from certain moving sexual parts: afterwards the celebrated marriage of Proserpina (with Pluto) takes place; and those who are initiated sing:

"'Out of the drum I have eaten,
Out of the cymbal I have drank,
The mystic vase I have sustained,
The bed I have entered.'

The pregnant throes likewise of Ceres [Deo] are represented: hence the supplications of Deo are exhibited; the drinking of bile, and the heart-aches. After this, an effigy with the thighs of a goat makes its appearance, which is represented as suffering vehemently about the testicles: because Jupiter, as if to expiate the violence which he had offered to Ceres, is represented as cutting off the testicles of a goat, and placing them on her bosom, as if they were his own. But after all this, the rites of Bacchus succeed; the Cista, and the cakes with many bosses, like those of a shield. Likewise the mysteries of Sabazius, divinations, and the mimalons or Bacchants; a certain sound of the Thesprotian bason; the Dodonæan brass; another Corybas, and another Proserpina,—representations of Demons. After these succeed the uncovering of the thighs of Baubo, and a woman's comb (*kteis*), for thus, through a sense of shame, they denominate the sexual parts of a woman. And thus, with scandalous exhibitions, they finish the initiation."

From this curious passage, it appears that the Eleusinian Mysteries comprehended those of almost all the gods; and this account will not only throw light on the relation of the Mysteries given by Clemens Alexandrinus, but likewise be elucidated by it in several particulars. I would willingly unfold to the reader the mystic meaning of the whole of this machinery, but this can not be accomplished by any one, without at least the possession of all the Platonic manuscripts which are extant. This acquisition, which I would infinitely prize above the wealth of the Indies, will, I hope, speedily and fortunately be mine, and then I shall be no less anxious to communicate this arcane information, than the liberal reader will be to receive it. I shall only therefore observe, that the mutual communication of energies among the gods was called by ancient theologists ἱερος γαμος, *hieros gamos, a sacred marriage;* concerning which Proclus, in the second book of his manuscript Commentary on the *Parmenides*, admirably remarks as follows:

Jupiter disguised as Diana, and Calisto.

Hercules, Deianeira and Nessus.

Ταυτην δε την κοινωνιαν, ποτε μεν εν τοις συστοιχοις ὁρωσι θεοις (οἱ θεολογοι) και καλουσι γαμον Ἡρας και Διος, Ουρανου και Γης, Κρονου και ῾Ρεας· ποτε δε των καταδεεστερων προς τα κρειττω, και καλουσι γαμον Διος και Δημητρας· ποτε δε και εμπαλιν των κρειττωνων προς τα ὑφειμενα, και λεγουσι Διος και Κορης γαμον. Επειδη των Θεων αλλαι μεν εισιν αἱ προς τα συστοιχα κοινωνιαι, αλλαι δε αἱ προς τα προ αυτων· αλλαι δε αἱ προς τα μετα ταυτα. Και δει την ἑκαστης ιδιοτητα κατανοειν και μεταγειν απο των Θεων επι τα ειδη την τοιαυτην διαπλοκην. *l. e.* "Theologists at one time considered this communion of the gods in divinities co-ordinate with each other; and then they called it the marriage of Jupiter and Juno, of Heaven and Earth [Uranos and Ge], of Saturn and Rhea: but at another time, they considered it as subsisting between subordinate and superior divinities; and then they called it the marriage of Jupiter and Ceres; but at another time, on the contrary, they beheld it as subsisting between superior and subordinate divinities; and then they called it the marriage of Jupiter and Koré. For in the gods there is one kind of communion between such as are of a co-ordinate nature; another between the subordinate and supreme; and another again between the supreme and subordinate. And it is necessary to understand the peculiarity of each, and to transfer a conjunction of this kind from the gods to the communion of ideas with each other."

And in *Timæus*, book i., he observes: και το την αυτην (supple θεαν) ἑτεροις ἢ τον αυτον θεον πλειοσι συζευγνυσθαι, λαβοις αν εκ των μυστικων λογων, και των εν απορρητοις λεγομενων ἱερων γαμων. *l. e.* "And that the same goddess is conjoined with other gods, or the same god with many goddesses, may be collected from the mystic discourses, and those marriages which are called in the Mysteries *Sacred Marriages*."

Thus far the divine Proclus; from the first of which passages the reader may perceive how adultery and rapes, as represented in the machinery of the Mysteries, are to be understood when applied to the gods; and that they mean nothing more than a communication of divine energies, either between a superior and subordinate, or subordinate and superior, divinity. I only add that the apparent indecency of these exhibitions was, as I have already observed, exclusive of its mystic meaning, designed as a remedy for the passions of the soul: and hence mystic ceremonies were very properly called ακεα, *akea, medicines*, by the obscure and noble Heracleitus. [135]

Sacrifice of a Pig.

FOOTNOTES

133. Dæmons, divinities, spirits; a term formerly applied to all rational beings, good or bad, other than mortals.
134. *I. e.* a representation of them.
135. IAMBLICHUS: *De Mysteriis*.

Orphic Hymns

Hercules Drunk.

l shall utter to whom it is lawful; but let the doors be closed,

Nevertheless, against all the profane. But do thou hear,

Oh Musæus, for l will declare what is true. . . .

He is the One, self-proceeding; and from him all things proceed,

And in them he himself exerts his activity; no mortal

Beholds Him, but he beholds all.

There is one royal body in which all things are enwombed,

Fire and Water, Earth, Æther, Night and Day,

And Counsel [*Metis*], the first producer, and delightful Love,—

For all these are contained in the great body of Zeus.

Zeus, the mighty thunderer, is first; Zeus is last;

Zeus is the head, Zeus the middle of all things;

From Zeus were all things produced. He is male, he is female;

Zeus is the depth of the earth, the height of the starry heavens;
He is the breath of all things, the force of untamed fire;
The bottom of the sea; Sun, Moon, and Stars;
Origin of all; King of all; One Power, one God, one Great Ruler.

Hymn of Cleanthes

Greatest of the gods, God with many names, God ever-ruling, and
ruling all things!

Zeus, origin of Nature, governing the universe by law,

All hail! For it is right for mortals to address thee;

For we are thy offspring, and we alone of all

That live and creep on earth have the power of imitative speech.

Therefore will I praise thee, and hymn forever thy power.

Thee the wide heaven, which surrounds the earth, obeys:

Following where thou wilt, willingly obeying thy law.

Thou holdest at thy service, in thy mighty hands,

The two-edged, flaming, immortal thunderbolt,

Before whose flash all nature trembles.

Thou rulest in the common reason, which goes through all,

And appears mingled in all things, great or small,

Which filling all nature, is king of all existences.

Nor without thee, Oh Deity, [136] does anything happen in the world,

From the divine ethereal pole to the great ocean,

Except only the evil preferred by the senseless wicked.

But thou also art able to bring to order that which is chaotic,

Giving form to what is formless, and making the discordant friendly;

So reducing all variety to unity, and even making good out of evil.

Thus throughout nature is one great law

Which only the wicked seek to disobey,

Poor fools! who long for happiness,

But will not see nor hear the divine commands.

[In frenzy blind they stray away from good,

By thirst of glory tempted, or sordid avarice,

Or pleasures sensual and joys that fall.]

But do thou, Oh Zeus, all-bestower, cloud-compeller!

Ruler of thunder! guard men from sad error.

Father! dispel the clouds of the soul, and let us follow

The laws of thy great and just reign!

That we may be honored, let us honor thee again,

Chanting thy great deeds, as is proper for mortals,

For nothing can be better for gods or men

Than to adore with hymns the Universal King. [137]

FOOTNOTES

136. Greek, Δαιμον, *Demon*,

137. Rev. J. Freeman Clarke, whose version is here copied, renders this phrase "the law common to all." The Greek text reads: "ἡ κοινον αει νομον εν δικη ὑμνειν,"—the term νομος, *nomos*, or Law, being used for King, as Love is for God.—A. W.

Proserpina Enthroned in Hades.

Nymphs and Centaurs.

Glossary

Aporrheta, Greek απορρητα—The instructions given by the hierophant or interpreter in the Eleusinian Mysteries, not to be disclosed on pain of death. There was said to be a synopsis of them in the *petroma* or two stone tablets, which, it is said, were bound together in the form of a book.

Apostatise—To fall or descend, as the spiritual part of the soul is said to descend from its divine home to the world of nature.

Cathartic—Purifying. The term was used by the Platonists and others in connection with the ceremonies of purification before initiation, also to the corresponding performance of rites and duties which renewed the moral life. The *cathartic* virtues were the duties and mode of living, which conduced to that end. The phrase is used but once or twice in this edition.

Cause—The agent by which things are generated or produced.

Circulation—The peculiar spiral motion or progress by which the spiritual nature or "intellect" descended from the divine region of the universe into the world of sense.

Cogitative—Relating to the understanding: dianoetic.

Conjecture, or *Opinion*—A mental conception that can be changed by argument.

Coré—A name of Ceres or Demeter, applied by the Orphic and later writers to her daughter Persephoné or Proserpina. She was supposed to typify the spiritual nature which was abducted by Hades or Pluto into the Underworld, the figure signifying the apostasy or descent of the soul from the higher life to the material body.

Corically—After the manner of Proserpina, *i. e.*, as if descending into death from the supernal world.

Dæmon—A designation of a certain class of divinities. Different authors employ the term differently. Hesiod regards them as the souls of the men who lived in the Golden Age, now acting as guardian or tutelary spirits. Socrates, in the *Cratylus*, says "that dæmon is a term denoting wisdom, and that every good man is dæmonian, both while living and when dead, and is rightly called a dæmon." His own attendant spirit that checked him whenever he endeavored to do what he might not, was styled his Dæmon. Iamblichus places Dæmons in the second order of spiritual existence.—Cleanthes, in his celebrated *Hymn*, styles Zeus δαιμον (*daimon*).

Demiurgus—The creator. It was the title of the; chief-magistrate in several Grecian States, and in this work is applied to Zeus or Jupiter, or the Ruler of the Universe. The latter Platonists, and more especially the Gnostics, who regarded matter as constituting or containing the principle of Evil, sometimes applied this term to the Evil Potency, who, some of them affirmed, was the Hebrew God.

Distributed—Reduced from a whole to parts and scattered. The spiritual nature or intellect in its higher estate was regarded as a whole, but in descending to worldly conditions became divided into parts or perhaps characteristics.

Divisible—Made into parts or attributes, as the mind, intellect, or spiritual, first a whole, became thus distinguished in its descent. This division was regarded as a fall into a lower plane of life.

Energise, Greek ενεργεω—To operate or work, especially to undergo discipline of the heart and character.

Energy—Operation, activity.

Eternal—Existing through all past time, and still continuing.

Faith—The correct conception of a thing as it seems,—fidelity.

Freedom—The ruling power of one's life; a power over what pertains to one's self in life.

Friendship—Union of sentiment; a communion in doing well.

Fury—The peculiar mania, ardor, or enthusiasm which inspired and actuated prophets, poets, interpreters of oracles, and others; also a title of the goddesses Demeter and Persephone as the chastisers of the wicked,—also of the Eumenides.

Generation, Greek γενεσις—Generated existence, the mode of life peculiar to this world, but which is equivalent to death, so far as the pure intellect or spiritual nature is concerned; the process by which the soul is separated from the higher form of existence, and brought into the conditions of life upon the earth. It was regarded as a punishment, and according to Mr. Taylor, was prefigured by the abduction of Proserpina. The soul is supposed to have pre-existed with God as a pure intellect like him, but not actually identical—at one but not absolutely the same.

Good—That which is desired on its own account.

Hades—A name of Pluto; the Underworld, the state or region of departed souls, as understood by classic writers; the physical nature, the corporeal existence, the condition of the soul while in the bodily life.

Herald, Greek κηρυξ—The crier at the Mysteries.

Hierophant—The interpreter who explained the purport of the mystic doctrines and dramas to the candidates.

Holiness, Greek ὁσιοτης—Attention to the honor due to God.

Idea—A principle in all minds underlying our cognitions of the sensible world.

Imprudent—Without foresight; deprived of sagacity.

Infernal regions—Hades, the Underworld.

Instruction—A power to cure the soul.

Intellect, Greek νους—Also rendered *pure reason*, and by Professor Cocker, *intuitive reason*, and the rational soul; the spiritual nature. "The organ of self-evident, necessary, and universal truth. In an immediate, direct, and intuitive manner, it takes hold on truth with absolute certainty. The reason, through the medium of *ideas*, holds communion with the world of real Being. These ideas are the *light* which reveals the world of unseen realities, as the sun reveals the world of sensible forms. '*The Idea of the good* is the *Sun* of the Intelligible World; it sheds on objects the light of truth, and gives to the soul that knows the power of knowing.' Under this light the eye of reason apprehends the eternal world of being as truly, yet more truly, than the eye of sense apprehends the world of phenomena. This power the rational soul possesses by virtue of its having a nature kindred, or even homogeneous with the Divinity. It was 'generated by the Divine Father,' and like him, it is in a certain sense 'eternal.' Not that we are to understand Plato as teaching that the rational soul had an independent and underived existence; it was created or 'generated' in eternity, and even now, in its incorporate state, is not amenable to the condition of time and space, but, in a peculiar sense, dwells in eternity: and therefore is capable of beholding eternal realities, and coming into communion with absolute beauty, and goodness, and truth—that is, with God, the *Absolute Being*."—*Christianity and Greek Philosophy*, x. pp. 349, 350.

Intellective—Intuitive; perceivable by spiritual insight.

Intelligible—Relating to the higher reason.

Interpreter—The hierophant or sacerdotal teacher who, on the last day of the Eleusinia, explained the *petroma* or stone book to the candidates, and unfolded the final meaning of the representations and symbols. In the Phoenician language he was called *peter*. Hence the *petroma*, consisting of two tablets of stone, was a pun on the designation, to imply the wisdom to be unfolded. It has been suggested by the Rev, Mr. Hyslop, that the Pope derived his claim, as the successor of Peter, from his succession to the rank and function of the Hierophant of the Mysteries, and not from the celebrated Apostle, who probably was never in Rome.

Just—Productive of Justice.

Justice—The harmony or perfect proportional action of all the powers of the soul, and comprising equity, veracity, fidelity, usefulness, benevolence, and purity of mind, or holiness.

Judgment—A peremptory decision covering a disputed matter; also διανοια, *dianoia*, or understanding.

Knowledge—A comprehension by the mind of fact not to be overthrown or modified by argument.

Legislative—Regulating.

Lesser Mysteries—The τελεται, *teletai*, or ceremonies of purification, which were celebrated at Agræ, prior to full initiation at Eleusis. Those initiated on this occasion were styled μυσται, *mystæ*, from μυω, *muo*, to vail; and their initiation was called μυησις, *muesis*, or vailing, as expressive of being vailed from the former life.

Magic—Persian *mag*, Sanscrit *maha*, great. Relating to the order of the Magi of Persia and Assyria.

Material dæmons—Spirits of a nature so gross as to be able to assume visible bodies like individuals still living on the Earth.

Matter—The elements of the world, and especially of the human body, in which the idea of evil is contained and the soul incarcerated. Greek ὑλη, *Hulé* or *Hylé*.

Muesis, Greek μυησις, from μυω, to vail—The last act in the Lesser Mysteries, or τελεται, *teletai*, denoting the separating of the initiate from the former exotic life.

Mysteries—Sacred dramas performed at stated periods. The most celebrated were those of Isis, Sabazius, Cybelè, and Eleusis.

Mystic—Relating to the Mysteries: a person initiated in the Lesser Mysteries—Greek μυσται.

Occult—Arcane; hidden; pertaining to the mystical sense.

Orgies, Greek οργιαι—The peculiar rites of the Bacchic Mysteries.

Opinion—A hypothesis or conjecture.

Partial—Divided, in parts, and not a whole.

Philologist—One pursuing literature.

Philosopher—One skilled in philosophy; one disciplined in a right life.

Philosophise—To investigate final causes; to undergo discipline of the life.

Philosophy—The aspiration of the soul after wisdom and truth, "Plato asserted philosophy to be the science of unconditioned being, and asserted that this was known to the soul by its intuitive reason (intellect or spiritual instinct) which is the organ of all philosophic insight. The reason perceives substance; the understanding, only phenomena. Being (το ον), which is the reality in all actuality, is in the ideas or thoughts of God; and nothing exists (or appears outwardly), except by the force of this indwelling idea. The WORD is the true expression of the nature of every object: for each has its divine and natural name, besides its accidental human appellation. Philosophy is the recollection of what the soul has seen of things and their names." (J. FREEMAN CLARKE.)

Plotinus—A philosopher who lived in the Third Century, and revived the doctrines of Plato.

Prudent—Having foresight.

Purgation, purification—The introduction into the *Teletæ* or Lesser Mysteries; a separation of the external principles from the soul.

Punishment—The curing of the soul of its errors.

Prophet, Greek μαντις,—One possessing the prophetic mania, or inspiration.

Priest—Greek μαντις—A prophet or inspired person, ἱερευς—a sacerdotal person.

Revolt—A rolling away, the career of the soul in its descent from the pristine divine condition.

Science—The knowledge of universal, necessary, unchangeable, and eternal ideas.

Shows—The peculiar dramatic representations of the Mysteries.

Teleté, Greek τελετη—The finishing or consummation; the Lesser Mysteries.

Theologist—A teacher of the literature relating to the gods.

Theoretical—Perceptive.

Torch bearer—A priest who bore a torch at the Mysteries.

Titans—The beings who made war against Kronos or Saturn. E. Pococke identifies them with the *Daityas* of India, who resisted the Brahmans. In the Orphic legend, they are described as slaying the child Bacchus-Zagreus.

Titanic—Relating to the nature of Titans.

Transmigration—The passage of the soul from one condition of being to another. This has not any necessary reference to any rehabilitation in a corporeal nature, or body of flesh and blood. See I *Corinthians*, XV.

Virtue—A good mental condition; a stable disposition.

Virtues—Agencies, rites, influences. *Cathartic Virtues*—Purifying rites or influences.

Wisdom—The knowledge of things as they exist; "the approach to God as the substance of goodness in truth."

World—The cosmos, the universe, as distinguished from the earth and human existence upon it.

Eleusinian Priest and Assistants.

Fortune and the Three Fates.

Supper-Scene.

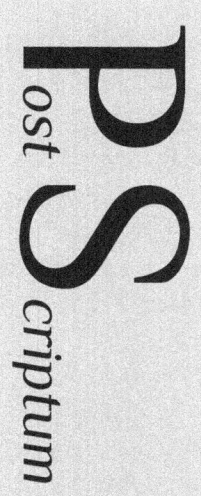

An admirer
of Hellenism

About Taylor

VAMzzz Publishing

Paper books

More Occult and Esoteric Books

Thomas Taylor

Thomas Taylor (15 May 1758 – 1 November 1835) was an English translator and Neoplatonist, the first to translate into English the complete works of Aristotle and of Plato, as well as the Orphic fragments. He was born in the City of London, the son of a staymaker, Joseph Taylor and his wife Mary (born Summers).

He received his education at St. Paul's School, and devoted himself to the study of the classics and of mathematics. After first working as a clerk in Lubbock's Bank, he was appointed Assistant Secretary to the Society for the Encouragement of Art (a precursor to the Royal Society of Arts), in which capacity he made many influential friends, who furnished the means for publishing his various translations, which besides Plato and Aristotle, include Proclus, Porphyry, Apuleius, Ocellus Lucanus and other Neoplatonists and Pythagoreans. His ambitious aim was the translation of all the un-translated writings of the ancient Greek philosophers. The texts that he used had been edited since the 16th century, but were interrupted by lacunae; Taylor's understanding of the Platonists informed his suggested emendations. His translations were influential on William Blake, Percy Bysshe Shelley and William Wordsworth. In American editions they were read by Ralph

Waldo Emerson, Bronson Alcott, and G. R. S. Mead, secretary to Helena Blavatsky of the Theosophical Society. Taylor also published several original works on philosophy (in particular, the Neoplatonism of Proclus and Iamblichus) and mathematics. These works have been republished (some for the first time since Taylor's lifetime) by the Prometheus Trust.

Taylor was an admirer of Hellenism, most specially in the philosophical framework furnished by Plato and the Neoplatonists Proclus and Iamblichus. So enamoured he was by the ancients, that he and his wife talked to one another only in classical Greek. Taylor made quite a few enemies by criticizing the corruption of Christianity of his days and was therefore ridiculed by them, but in other circles he was well respected. Among his friends he counted the eccentric traveller and philosopher John "Walking" Stewart, whose gatherings Taylor was in the habit of attending.

Taylor married his childhood sweetheart Mary Morton in 1777, and they had four sons, George Burrow Taylor (born 1779), John Buller Taylor (1781), William Grainger Taylor (1783) and Thomas Taylor (1791). Their daughter, Mary Meredith Taylor (1787–1861), was named after his generous patron William Meredith and married a haberdasher, Samuel Beverly Jones. It appears that he

'Taylor's ambitious aim was the translation of all the un-translated writings of the ancient Greek philosophers.'

and his wife were landlords at Walworth in the late 1770's to a family that included the 18-year-old Mary Wollstonecraft. His wife Mary died in 1809. He married again, and his second wife Susannah died in 1823. From his second marriage he had one son, Thomas Proclus Taylor (born 1816). Thomas Taylor died in Walworth.

Bibliography

1780: *The Elements of a New Method of Reasoning in Geometry, applied to the Rectification of the Circle*

1782: *Ocellus Lucanus on the Nature of the Universe* (see 1831 for later edition)

1787: *The Mystical Initiations or Hymns of Orpheus, with a preliminary Dissertation on the Life and Theology of Orpheus Concerning the Beautiful; or, a paraphrase translation from the Greek of Plotinus,* Ennead I. Book VI.

1788-89: *The Philosophical and Mathematical Commentaries of Proclus on the First Book of Euclid's Elements, and his Life by Marinus.* With a preliminary Dissertation on the Platonic Doctrine of Ideas. To which are added A History of the Restoration of the Platonic Theology by the later Platonists, 2 vols. (see 1792 for second revised edition)

1790: *A Dissertation on the Eleusinian and Bacchic Mysteries*

1792: *A Vindication of the Rights of Brutes The Phædrus of Plato: A Dialogue Concerning Beauty and Love An Essay on the Beautiful, from the Greek of Plotinus The Philosophical and Mathematical Commentaries of Proclus on the First Book of Euclid's Elements, and his Life by Marinus.* With a preliminary Dissertation on the Platonic Doctrine of Ideas. To which are added A History of the Restoration of the Platonic Theology by the later Platonists, 2 vols.

1793: *Sallust on the Gods and the World, and the Pythagoric Sentences of Demophilus, and Five Hymns by Proclus; to which are added Five Hymns by the translator.* Two Orations of the Emperor Julian, one to the Sovereign Sun, and the other to the Mother of the Gods; with Notes and a copious Introduction Four Dialogues of Plato: The Cratylus, Phædo, Parmenides and Timæus.

1794: *Pausanias's Description of Greece* (see 1824 for second edition, enlarged) *Five Books of Plotinus, viz. On Felicity; on the Nature and Origin of Evil; on Providence; on Nature, Contemplation, and the One; and on the Descent of the Soul.*

1795: *The Fable of Cupid and Psyche;* to which are added a Poetical
Paraphrase on the Speech of Diotima in the Banquet of Plato;
Four Hymns, With an Introduction, in which the meaning of the
Fable is unfolded.

1801: *Aristotle's Metaphysics,* to which is added a Dissertation on
Nullities and Diverging Series

1803: *Hedric's Greek Lexicon* (Graecum Lexicon Manuale, primum a
Benjamine Hederico)

1804: *Four letters from Thomas Taylor, the Platonist, to Charles Taylor,*
Secretary of the Society of Arts, 1800-1804. An Answer to Dr.
Gillies's *Supplement to his New Analysis of Aristotle's Works The
Dissertations of Maximus Tyrius,* 2 vols. *The Works of Plato, viz.
His Fifty-Five Dialogues and Twelve Epistles,* 5 vols.

1805: *Miscellanies in Prose and Verse, containing the Triumph of the
Wise Man over Fortune according to the doctrine of the Stoics and
Platonists; the Creed of the Platonic Philosopher; a Panegyric on
Sydenham* (see 1820 for 2nd Edition, with additions)

1806: *Collectanea; or Collections consisting of Miscellanies inserted in the
European and Monthly Magazines.* With an Appendix containing
some Hymns never before printed.

1807: *The Treatises of Aristotle on the Heavens* (see also v.7 of The Works
of Aristotle, 1812)

1809: *The Elements of the true Arithmetic of Infinites. In which all the
Propositions on the Arithmetic of Infinites invented by Dr. Wallis
relative to the summation of fluxions are demonstrated to be false,
and the nature of infinitesimals is unfolded. The History of Animals
of Aristotle and his Treatise on Physiognomy* (see also v.8 of *The
Works of Aristotle,* 1812) *The Arguments of the Emperor Julian
against the Christians, to which are added Extracts from the other
Works of Julian relative to the Christians.*

1810: *The Commentaries of Proclus on the Timæus of Plato* (see 1820 for
2nd edition)

1811: *The Rhetoric, Poetic and Nicomachean Ethics of Aristotle* (see 1818
for 2nd edition)

1812: *The Works of Aristotle, with copious Elucidations from the best of his Greek Commentators,* 9 vols. A Dissertation on the Philosophy of Aristotle

1816: *A Dissertation on the Eleusinian and Bacchic Mysteries* (2nd Edition) *Theoretic Arithmetic,* in three books, containing the substance of all that has been written on this subject by Theo of Smyrna, Nicomachus, Iamblicus, and Boetius. *The Six Books of Proclus, the Platonic Successor,* on the Theology of Plato, 2 vols.

1817: *Remarks on the Dæmon of Socrates* (article) *Use of Arches Known Among the Ancients* (article) *Select Works of Plotinus, and Extracts from the Treatise of Synesius on Providence. With an Introduction containing the substance of Porphyry's Life of Plotinus*

1818: *Collection of the Chaldean Oracles* (articles) *Orphic Fragments, hitherto inedited* (article) *Remarks on the Passage in Stobæus* (article) *On a Peculiar Signification of the words Demas and Soma* (article) *The Rhetoric, Poetic and Nicomachean Ethics of Aristotle* (2nd Edition), 2 vols. *Iamblichus' Life of Pythagoras or Pythagoric Life, accompanied by fragments of the Ethical Writings of certain Pythagoreans in the Doric Dialect, and a Collection of Pythagoric Sentences from Stobæus and Others*

1819: *On the Philosophical Meaning of the words Bios, Kimena, Energema, and Sisthema* (article) *On the Antiquity of Alchymy* (article) *On the Coincidence between the Belts of the Planet Jupiter and the Fabulous Bonds of Jupiter the Demiurgus* (article)

1820: *Important Additions to the first Alcibiades, and Timæus of Plato* (article) *Important Discovery of the Original of many of the Sentences of Sextus Pythagoricus* (article) *Discovery of a Verse of Homer, and Error of Kiessling* (article) *Platonic Demonstration of the Immortality of the Soul* (article) *On the Theology of the Greeks* (article) *Miscellanies in Prose and Verse, containing the Triumph of the Wise Man over Fortune according to the doctrine of the Stoics and Platonists; the Creed of the Platonic Philosopher; a Panegyric on Sydenham* (2nd Edition, with additions) *The Commentaries of Proclus on the Timæus of Plato* (2nd Edition), 2 vols.

1821: *On the Mythology of the Greeks* (article) *Notice of Professor Cousin's edition of the two first books of Proclus on the Parmenides of Plato* (article) *Iamblichus on the Mysteries of the Egyptians, Chaldeans, and Assyrians.*

1822: *Observations on Professor Cousin's edition of the Commentaries of Proclus on the first Alcibiades of Plato* (article) *Observations on that part of a work entitled Empedoclis et Parmenidis Fragmenta* (article) *The Metamorphosis, or Golden Ass, and Philosophical Works of Apuleius Political Fragments of Archytas, Charondas, Zaleucus, and other ancient Pythagoreans, preserved by Stobæus, and also Ethical Fragments of Hierocles,* the celebrated commentator on the Pythagoric verses preserved by the same author.

1823: *The Elements of a new Arithmetical Notation and of a new Arithmetic of Infinites Observations on the Creuzer's edition of the Commentary of Olypiodorus on the first Alcibiades of Plato* (article) *Observations on the Scholia of Hermeas on the Phædrus of Plato* (article) *Select Works of Porphyry, containing his Four Books on Abstinence from Animal Food; his Treatise on the Homeric Cave of the Nymphs, and his Auxiliaries to the perception of Intelligible Natures.* With an Appendix explaining the Allegory of the Wanderings of Ulysses.

1824: *Emendations of the text of Plato* (article) *Observations on the Excerpta from the Scholia of Proclus on the Cratylus of Plato* (article) *The Mystical Hymns of Orpheus, demonstrated to be the Invocations which were used in the Eleusinian Mysteries, with Considerable Emendations, Alterations, and Additions. The Description of Greece by Pausanias,* 2nd edition with considerable augmentations, 3 vols.

1825: *Classical Allusion* [to Democrates] (article) *Notice of Professor Cousin's edition of the third, fourth and fifth books of Proclus on the Parmenides of Plato* (article) *Biblical Criticism* (article) *The Fragments that remain of the Lost Writings of Proclus.*

1829: *Corruption of Demiurgus* (article) *Extracts from some of the Lost*

Works of Aristotle, Xenocrates, and Theophrastus (article)

1830: *Arguments of Celsus, Porphyry, and the Emperor Julian, against the Christians*

1831: *Ocellus Lucanus on the Nature of the Universe. Taurus, the Platonic Philosopher, on the Eternity of the World; Julius Firmicus Maternus of the Thema Mundi, in which the positions of the stars at the commencement of the several mundane periods is (sic) given; Select Theorems on the Perpetuity of Time by Proclus.*

1833: *Two Treatises of Proclus, the Platonic Successor, the former consisting of ten Doubts concerning Providence, and a Solution of those Doubts, and the latter containing a Development of the Nature of Evil.*

1834: *Translations from the Greek of the following treatises of Plotinus: On Suicide, to which is added an Extract from the Harl. MS. of the Scholia of Olympiodorus on the Phædo of Plato respecting Suicide. Two Books on Truly Existing Being, and Extracts from his Treatise on the manner in which the multitude of ideas subsists, and concerning the Good, with additional Notes from Porphyry and Proclus.*

Paper books

VAMzzz Publishing is located in the very centre of old Amsterdam, in The Netherlands. Our publishing company creates high quality revised editions of five star occult, witchcraft, Gothic and esoteric classics, mostly written in the Fin de siècle-period and early 20th century.

As a publisher, we deeply respect the writer of any book we choose, so we join our forces (top level graphic design & thirty years of occult studies) to produce enchanting volumes which maximize the reading pleasure and inform, often with extra added information. In contrast to the current trend of digital screen addiction, we think, this variety of literature needs to be presented on paper. *No e-books, but real books!*

Apart from re-publications of valuable but forgotten books, we are also in the preparation of new publications on topics such as self-healing, magic, new astrology and more.

Previews of all books including a complete table of contents can be viewed on www.vamzzz.com. More books will be added to the list. Please visit our website regularly for the latest updates.

VAMzzz Publishing
P.O. Box 3340
1001 AC Amsterdam
The Netherlands
contactvamzzz@gmail.com
www.vamzzz.com

Recommended

PAN Magazine
by VAMzzz Publishing
Free Online
www.vamzzz.com/pan.html

In Greek religion and mythology, PAN, the companion of the nymphs, is the god of the wild, shepherds and flocks, wild mountains and rustic music. He has the hindquarters, legs and horns of a goat, in the same manner as a faun or satyr. He is also recognized as the god of fields, groves and wooded glens; connected to fertility, the joy of life itself and the season of spring.

Though a mortal god in antiquity and an underground witch-god in medieval times, the last decades PAN has become a patron of both modern occultism, Wicca, paganism and the green guerilla – enthroned again as the one and only God of the Earth and Nature. PAN is the vibe touching those who refuse to become part of a machine, and who remain loyal to Mother Nature, the visible and hidden one. Therefore PAN is the most suitable icon we could chose for this periodical.

The Banshee
A Ghost Hunter's Investigation
by Elliot O'Donnell
222 pages, Paperback, ISBN 9789492355232

The banshee is a mysterious female spirit in Irish folklore, who heralds the death of a family member, usually by shrieking or keening. The screeching sound is described as somewhere between the wail of a woman and the moan of an owl, a low singing or piercing loud and able to break glass. The banshee appears as an old hag or beautiful lady, but may also appear as a crow, stoat, hare and weasel - animals associated in Ireland with witchcraft.

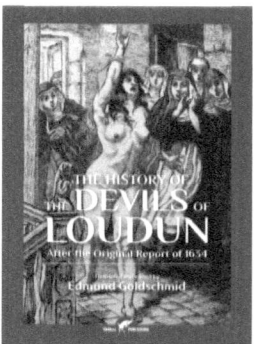

The History of the Devils of Loudun
After the Original Report of 1634
Translation by Edmund Goldschmid
118 pages, Paperback, ISBN 9789492355256

Around 1632 seventeen Ursuline Nuns were taken over by demons and went into a sexual and blasphemous state of hysteria for years. The work also describes the trial of a womanizing local priest named Father Urbain Grandier, who was accused of summoning these demons and, in the end, burned at the stake.

Religion and Lust
or The Physical Correlation of Religious Emotion and Sexual Desire
by James Weir Jr.
146 pages, Paperback, ISBN 9789492355270

In *Religion and Lust,* author James Weir Jr. investigates the origins of religious feeling, the once world wide spread fertility worship and the physical correlation of religious emotion and sexual desire. A major part of the work is filled with a colourful collection of religious or semi-religious, sexual rites, once practiced all over the globe, connecting the most "primitive" tribe to the most "civilized" nations.

Incubi and Succubi or Demoniality
A Historical Study of Sexual Contacts with Demons
by Sinistrari of Ameno
194 pages, Paperback, ISBN 9789492355263

This book is a revised English edition of Sinistrari's fascinating 17th century study on the orgasm-stimulating sex demon. The incubus and succubus are the same creature. The incubus is its male shape, copulates with women. The succubus visits men, triggering wet dreams. The intercourse with this astral visitor was called demoniality, a term no longer in use, though nowadays people are still having these mysterious incubus/succubus-"sexperiences".

Mysteria
History of the Secret Doctrines & Mystic Rites of Ancient Religions & Medieval and Modern Secret Orders
by Dr. Otto Henne am Rhyn
288 pages, Paperback, ISBN 9789492355225

Mysteria is a treasure box of missing conspiracy links and one of the very few publications, which offer reliable information about Adam Weishaupt's Illuminati for "the web & media-disinformed". Lodge-insider Otto Henne am Rhyn takes you on a journey, back to the Mystery cults of ancient Egypt, Babylon and Greece, passes Templars and explains modern lodges.

Magic and Magical Fetish
by Alfred Cort Haddon
108 pages, Paperback, ISBN 9789492355300

Alfred C. Haddon gives a practical and theoretical insight of the universal principles of magic, categorized in different techniques. The book is one of the very few works ever published, which describes wind and rain making. Magic is divided into sympathetic magic, the magic of words, talismans and divination, magical training routines. A kaleidoscope of forgotten magical techniques, which wasn't available for decades.

The Eleusian and Bacchic Mysteries
A Dissertation
by Thomas Taylor
200 pages, Paperback, ISBN 9789492355294

The Eleusian and Bacchic Mysteries focus on life, death and rebirth in a living nature (the present), while this nature was regarded as the converging of past and future. Taylor describes a series of lost secret rites. These rites were once the appointed means for regeneration through an inner union with the Divine Essence, despite their wild and sexual aspect.

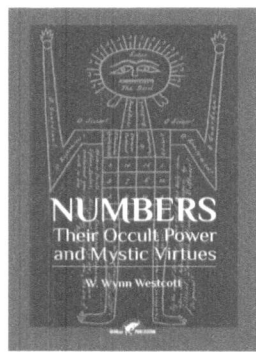

Numbers
Their Occult Power and Mystic Virtues
by W. Wynn Westcott
170 pages, Paperback, ISBN 9789492355287

This book may be regarded as the "bible of numerology". It deals with Pythagorean number divisions, explains 3 different kinds of Kabalistic numerology, and reveals the hidden logic and symbolism of the numbers 1,2,3,4,5,6,7,8,9,10,11,12 and 13. This is accompanied by a long course of numbers between 14 and 25920. Special symbolisms are included like the link between numbers and planets and numbers in relation to the Apocalypse.

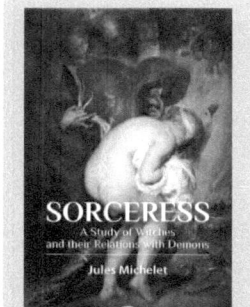

Sorceress
A Study of Witches and their Relations with Demons
by Jules Michelet
432 pages, Paperback, ISBN 9789492355249

This work is one of the most vivid, dark and confronting studies on witchcraft ever produced. Long before Murray's Witch-Cult in Western Europe, Michelet positions the medieval witch within a diminishing ancient culture of nature worship and the ruthless efforts of Christianity, with its cruel hostility towards nature, life (and women), to overwrite it. A nightmare of the most extraordinary verisimilitude and poetical power...

Aradia
Gospel of the Witches
by Charles Godfrey Leland
174 pages, Paperback, ISBN 9789492355010

This wonderful book describes the creation according to Italian witch-lore. We also read about the witch-meeting or sabbath (treguenda) and the book contains many original magical recipes, like spells for love and good fortune. Diana is further connected to the Moon and the fairy world.

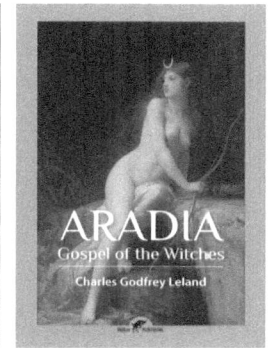

Demonology and Devil-Lore *(Volume 1)*
by Moncure Daniel Conway
490 pages, Paperback, ISBN 9789492355157

Demonology and Devil-Lore *(Volume 2)*
by Moncure Daniel Conway
518 pages, Paperback, ISBN 9789492355164

Within the demonology scope, this rare and mostly forgotten, almost 1000 pages thick masterpiece, remains unsurpassed in quality and completeness. Even in the 21st century the works offer fascinating missing links for both the academic and student of occult traditions. Moncure Daniel Conway divides Volume 1 in three parts and deals mainly with the evolution and thematic classification of ex-gods, demons and nature creatures. Volume 2 deals primarily with the diabolic and with the Devil himself, his ethnic history and connected topics.

Fairy Mythology *(Volume 1)*
Romance and Superstition of Various Countries 1
by Thomas Keightley
404 pages, Paperback, ISBN 9789492355096

Fairy Mythology *(Volume 2)*
Romance and Superstition of Various Countries 2
by Thomas Keightley
404 pages, Paperback, ISBN 9789492355102

The term Fairy covers all kinds of nature spirits, not just the tiny sugarsweet creatures hovering around flowers. A unique and impressive book on this subject, published in a revised 2 volume-edition. No wiccan or pagan can afford to leave these books unopened. About Elves, Dwarfs, Kobolds, Trolls, Changelings, Meremaids, Nisses, Fairies, Brownies, Puck and other Elemental spirits all over the world.

Etruscan Magic & Occult Remedies
(Two volumes in one book)
by Charles Godfrey Leland
628 pages, Paperback, ISBN 9789492355003

Part One of the book gives us a complete and detailed insight in the Etruscan and Roman rooted pantheon of the Tuscan Streghe (witches). Part Two describes many of their spells, incantations, sorcery and several lost divination methods. Much information in this book, Leland received first hand from the Tuscan witches Maddalena and Marietta.

Voodoos and Obeahs
Phases of West India Witchcraft
by Joseph J. Williams
374 pages, Paperback, ISBN 9789492355119

This work goes into great depth concerning the New
World-African connection and is highly recommended if
you want a deep understanding of the dramatic historical
background of Haitian and Jamaican magic and witchcraft,
and the profound influence of imperialism, slavery and
racism on its development. Williams includes numerous
quotations from rare documents and books on the topic.

Devil-worship in France
Or The Question of Lucifer
by Arthur Edward Waite
240 pages, Paperback, ISBN 9789492355065

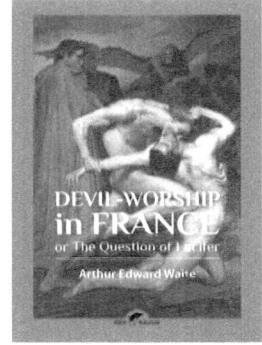

In *Devil-Worship in France,* Waite attempts to discern
what is genuine from what is fake in the evidence of
19th century Satanism. To get the answers he spends
a great deal of time investigating the French Masonic
echelon, debunking a "conspiracy of falsehood" and
determining what should be understood by Satanism
and what not. Huysmans' diabolical novel *Là-Bas*
(1891) inspired Waite to write this sceptical analysis.

Testament of Solomon
A First Century AD Grimoire
76 pages, Paperback, ISBN 9789492355041

A first century AD grimoire, and therefore the oldest,
and least known, of all grimoires (magical instruction
books) in the occult tradition. The book describes
health inflicting demons of zodiacal decans, summoned
by King Solomon, and how he controlled them to use
their forces to build his temple and more. Translated by
F. C. Conybeare, appeared first in the *Jewish Quarterly
Review* of October, 1898.

Ophiolatreia
Rites and Mysteries of Serpent Worship
by Hargrave Jennings
186 pages, Paperback, ISBN 9789492355126

An account of the rites and mysteries connected with the origin, rise and development of serpent worship in various parts of the world, enriched with interesting traditions, and a full description of the celebrated serpent mounds & temples, the whole forming an exposition of one of the phases of phallic, or sex worship.

Anansi
Jamaican stories of the Spider God
by Martha Warren Beckwith
494 pages, Paperback, ISBN 9789492355171

Anansi is both a god, spirit and African folktale character. He often takes the shape of a spider and is considered to be the spirit of all knowledge of stories. He is also one of the most important characters of West African and Caribbean folklore.

Spiritual Fetichism
A Study of West African Culture, Witchcraft, Magic & Demonology
by Robert Hamill Nassau
524 pages, Paperback, ISBN 9789492355188

Despite a nowadays anachronist and disturbing perspective, the book has remained most valuable for students of the occult, especially those interested in demonology, voodoo, hoodoo and its roots, African magick and religion, witchcraft, the classes of African spirits, and of course the spiritual and magickal use of a fetish.

Là-Bas
A Journey into the Self
by Joris-Karl Huysmans
378 pages, Paperback, ISBN 9789492355058

The plot of *Là-Bas* concerns the novelist Durtal, who is disgusted by the emptiness and vulgarity of the modern world. He seeks relief by turning to the study of the Middle Ages. Through his contacts in Paris, Durtal discovers that Satanism is not a thing of the past but alive and kicking in turn of the century France. The novel culminates with a description of a black mass.

Unicorn
A mythological investigation
by Robert Brown Jr.
124 pages, Paperback, ISBN 9789492355072

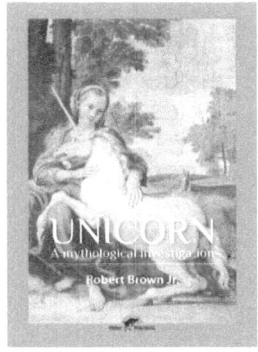

Brown Jr. believes the unicorn to be a lunar symbol, and draws on mythology from a wide range of sources all over the world to build his case. The author discusses the heraldic use of the unicorn, relates the creature to ancient goddesses like Astarte, Hecate en the Gorgon Medusa, and provides the reader with lost esoteric Moon-lore.

The House of Souls
A Fragment of Life / The White People
The Great God Pan / The Inmost Light
by Arthur Machen
336 pages, Paperback, ISBN 9789492355218

A collection of four masterpieces of horror and mystery, first collectively published in 1906. In the ingenious plot of *The Great God Pan,* a young woman is forced into Pan's reality, and turns into a femme fatale. *The Inmost Light* involves a doctor's scientific experiments into occultism and a vampiric force. In *The White People* a young girl's diary is discovered, describing her initiation into a secret world of folklore and ritual magic. In *A Fragment of Life* Machen tries to convince us of a hidden reality.

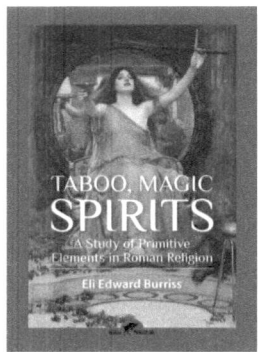

Taboo, Magic, Spirits
A study of primitive elements in Roman religion
by Eli Edward Burriss
200 pages, Paperback, ISBN 9789492355034

In Ancient Rome Mana was the term used for a mysterious, magical medium, which could be helpful or harmful (Taboo). Just like the Chinese qi, it could empower the positive and the negative. Contents: Mana, Magic and Animism – Positive and Negative Mana (Taboo) – Miscellaneous Taboos – Magic Acts: The General Principles – Removing Evils by - Magic Acts – Incantation and Prayer– Naturalism and Animism.

Chaldean Magic
It's Origin and Development
by François Lenormant
454 pages, Paperback, ISBN 9789492355027

The essentials of magic in Chaldea are presented inside a context of comparison or contrast to Egyptian, Median, Turanian, Finno-Tartarian and Akkadian magic, mythologies, religion and speech. Interesting is the Chaldean demonology, with its incubus, succubus, vampire, nightmare and many Elemental spirits, most of them coalesced with the primal powers of nature.

Amazons - Two publications in one book -
I. *The Amazons* by Guy Cadogan Rothery
II. *Religious Cults Associated With the Amazons*
   by Florence Mary Bennett
328 pages, Paperback, ISBN 9789492355089

Contents I: The Amazons of Antiquity – Amazons in Far Asia – Modern Amazons of the Caucasus – Amazons of Europe – Amazons of Africa – Amazons of America – The Amazon Stones. Contents II: The Amazons in Greek legend – The Great Mother – Ephesian Artemis – Artemis Astrateia and Apollo Amazonius – Ares.

www.ingramcontent.com/pod-product-compliance
Lightning Source LLC
Chambersburg PA
CBHW020243130626
46549CB00005B/2031